# WORKPLACE WARFARE

## HOW TO SURVIVE INCOMPETENT COLLEAGUES, HORRIBLE BOSSES AND ORGANIZATIONAL THEATRICS

### YASSER MATTAR, PHD

Copyright © 2015 by Yasser Mattar

Printed by CreateSpace, an Amazon.com company

ISBN-13: 978-1515085645

ISBN-10: 1515085643

http://twitter.com/workplacewar

ALL RIGHTS RESERVED. No part of this publication may be reproduced or transmitted in any form or by any means, electronic or mechanical, including photocopying, recording, or any other information storage and retrieval system, without the written permission of the author.

Cover illustrations by Dian Lestari & Ivan Danny Handoko

# FIND YOUR BEARINGS...

Preface ................................................................................................5

Introduction .......................................................................................6

CHAPTER 1: How to Survive Incompetent Colleagues .............27

   Types of Colleagues ...................................................................28

      The Gossipmonger ................................................................29

      The Whisperer .......................................................................32

      The Keyboard Warrior ..........................................................34

      The Mouse .............................................................................37

      The Captains of Incompetence ............................................40

      Caveat Lector ........................................................................45

   Declaration of War .....................................................................48

   Making Alliances .......................................................................56

   The Non-Competitive Ones ......................................................59

   Checkpoint One .........................................................................63

CHAPTER 2: How to Survive Horrible Bosses ............................65

   The Managerial Imperative .......................................................66

   Types of Managers .....................................................................70

      The Machiavellian Manager .................................................71

      The Bross ...............................................................................74

      The Simulator ........................................................................77

      The Artful Dodger .................................................................80

      Caveat Lector ........................................................................84

   Sandwiched Managers ...............................................................90

   Managing Management .............................................................94

- Group Preservation ................................................................. 95
- Fighting Capabilities ............................................................. 101
- Manager-Staffer Alliances .................................................... 106
- Management as Mediator ................................................... 110
- Checkpoint Two ...................................................................... 115
- CHAPTER 3: How to Survive Organizational Theatrics ........... 118
  - The Work Process ................................................................. 126
  - Work-Life Balance ................................................................ 134
  - One Big Happy Family ........................................................ 139
  - Job Interviews ...................................................................... 147
  - Giving Suggestions ............................................................. 156
  - Diversity ................................................................................. 159
  - Checkpoint 3 ......................................................................... 164
- Conclusion ................................................................................... 167
- About the Author ....................................................................... 176
- References .................................................................................. 177

# PREFACE

Every morning when you walk into the workplace, you watch your step for landmines. Every time you pop your head up above your cubicle, you see arrows flying in your direction. You duck, just to avoid them. Fearing for your safety, you dig a foxhole and bury yourself in it for the next nine hours. At the end of the day, when you walk out of the workplace, you thank your lucky stars that you came out alive.

The workplace is a war zone. Which side will you choose?

Do you want to be the likeable colleague who gets along with everyone? Do you want to just put your head down, work hard and maximize your potential? Do you want to be the best team player you can be?

Then this book is NOT for you.

This book is for those of us who have always wondered…

* Why the reward for good work is usually more work…

* Why good work never really seems to speak for itself…

* Why incompetence seems to be tolerated at the workplace…

* Why some people never really put in their full effort at work…

* Why workplaces are so fond of calling themselves "family"…

* Why some people just don't bother with office politics, while others are absolutely in the thick of it…

If this whets your appetite, please read on. I repeat. The workplace is a war zone, and we do what we must to survive. Lock and load.

# INTRODUCTION

All is fair in love and war. But nothing is quite fair in the workplace. Come on. We all do what we have to do to make a living. We like our jobs to varying degrees. Some of us absolutely love our jobs, while others among us just tolerate them. I mean, we're all fairly good at our jobs. Not perfect, but fairly good.

Some of us work just because we need the money. If this describes us, then we pretty much love the money, but not so much everything else about the job. We celebrate our monthversaries with the job and fall in love with the job over and over again. On payday, just in case you didn't get what I was getting at.

But hey, some of us aren't in it just for the money, and we work because we feel passionately for the profession. Really, I mean some of us are quite comfortable with our material lives and thus don't need any extra money beyond what we we're getting. Affluent, yes we are, but more importantly, we evaluate our jobs based on the satisfaction we get from the job. Money to some of us, is a hygiene factor. We will be unhappy and uncomfortable without it, but money in and of itself does not motivate us to give our best at work. As previously argued by Frederick Herzberg, the challenge of the work, the recognition for work well done, the opportunity to do meaningful tasks and such are more important to us because these give us a feeling of satisfaction from our jobs, and consequently, motivation to perform.

And then there are those of us who don't need the money at all and work for sheer passion. Retirees, for example. Some retirees come out of retirement and assume positions just because they feel passionately for the profession. Young people with rich parents, for example. Their parents might give them some cash to open a small bohemian boutique or a hipster cafe or something. They pretty much work just for passion, not for the money.

Of course, there are the odd hedons who don't work but would rather choose to surf or ride motorcycles or play acoustic folk songs their whole lives.

Most of us are toggling in between all of these categories mentioned above. On some days, we come to work full of passion and don't mind not claiming that inconsequential taxi fare. On other days, particularly when we're frustrated with our jobs, we're counting the days to payday and continually tell ourselves that we're just in this job for the money. Yet, on other days, we wish we could just run away and join a hippie commune away from the hustle and bustle of the rat race.

Let's face it. Work is unnatural. Can we imagine our Paleolithic forefathers being woken up ever so rudely by a blaring alarm clock, then splashing themselves with water, then deliberately putting stinging alcohol on their faces, then rushing off, all at the same time, towards a cave where they would sit and toil for the next nine hours or more? No? But that's exactly what we do today. Sounds strange when put in that context, doesn't it? The anthropologist Horace Minor previously painted a similar scenario for us. He described the strange rituals of a tribe he calls as the Nacirema, but as it was revealed to us at the end of his article, he was actually describing Americans (Nacirema spelled backwards).

Why do we do this to ourselves? For the reasons I made above. We seek money and satisfaction from this activity called "work".

If we were to follow our natural instincts, we'd rise when there is a need to rise. We'd shower when we're dirty. And we certainly wouldn't squeeze into an overcrowded train carriage or sit in traffic just to get to somewhere we don't absolutely have to be anyway.

And yet, when we get to the workplace, which we've fought tooth and nail to get to through the unforgiving traffic and irreverent trains, mind you, we find that it ain't all that fair. We find ourselves thinking, "I got out of bed just for this?" That was how I began this book anyway. Now, I beg my own question, why not? Why is nothing quite fair in the workplace?

Well, firstly, none of us are clones of each other. We each bring a little something something to the table in the workplace. We each bring along our respective knowledge and skills. Some of this was gained from previous jobs. Some of this was gained from formal education. And so we all try (to varying degrees) to contribute some level of usefulness (debatable, I agree) to the work process. And that little something something that we bring to the table includes a little bit of attitude as well. We all have different attitudes towards the workplace (this is covered in Chapter 2 under "Types of Colleagues"). Some of us are, well, not so motivated. For many reasons, motivation is kind of lost on some of us. Not that there's anything wrong with us, you see. As Peter Gibbons said in the cult classic *Office Space*, "It's not that I'm lazy, it's that I just don't care... It's a problem of motivation, alright?" Motivation is the result of a variety of different factors, some within our control and some without. Others among us are not that great at our jobs and are just trying to wing it. Don't lie. You know who you are. I'm guilty of that too. There was once I was asked to teach a class on medical psychology. Come on, I'm an organizational behaviorist. What in the world did I know about medical psychology? But just like a baker, I kneaded (needed, duh) the dough. So I winged it like a winger. 2 words. Wiki. Pedia.

Secondly, our relative ranks, appointments and positions in the workplace imbue us with different imperatives. And our relative ranks in our respective organizations are determined by the issue of "trust". New institutional economists like Oliver E. Williamson have looked at organizational cultures, and have argued that organizations often have "trust" issues with their employees. Organizations do not trust employees to not pilfer company assets. Organizations do not trust employees to not shame the company through their indiscretions. Organizations do not trust employees to deliver deliverables on time. And so how do organizations handle this trust issue? Organizations have chosen to go about it in two ways: Either to market out the tasks that need to be done to subcontractors, or to split the organization into a reporting hierarchical structure. Organizations which choose to market out the tasks that need to be done tend to remain small in employee size. They don't employ employees to do most of the work. Rather, they pay subcontractors to do most of their work for them. Does this work? For their intents and purposes, very much so! You see, subcontractors are primarily interested in earning money from their client organizations. The client organizations, in turn, are primarily interested in getting tasks done. The relationship between client organizations and subcontractors thus become a reciprocal "arm's length" relationship which works for both parties. The trust issue is thus overcome by paying for tasks to be done, while keeping the ones doing those tasks outside of the organization. The other way to address this trust issue would be to split the organization into a reporting hierarchical structure. This suits larger organizations much better. In this instance, the organization will put the least trustworthy fella at the very bottom of the hierarchy. He reports to somebody who reports to somebody who reports to somebody. The least trustworthy fella is of course, the lowest ranking Staffer. The higher up the hierarchy one goes, the more trustworthy the fellas get. Those at the bottom are checked by the ones above them. Those fellas higher up the top are given the title of "Management" and are vested with the powers of representing the organization. The ones in the middle, well, they're pretty much sandwiched in between the upper Management and the Staff. I refer to them as "Sandwiched Managers" in Chapter 2. These fellas often get the short end of the stick both ways. Staffers treat them like Managers, because they hold an official Managerial title. They're also required to defend the interests of the organization, which I will refer to, also in Chapter 2, as the "Managerial Imperative". Yet, their superior Managers think of them as not trustworthy enough to have significant decision-making powers and to effect change in the organization. In effect, these Sandwiched Managers are chimeras that have the worst of each parentage.

The greatest trick Management ever pulled was to convince Staff that rank doesn't exist. Some Managers are happy to have us recognize their superiority. These are the kind who will correct the way we refer to them. Remember that episode of *Seinfeld* where George Costanza's dad insists that George refer to him as "Mr Costanza" in the place of business? Yes, that's what I mean. But there are also some Managers who do not want the hierarchy acknowledged. Again, for a variety of reasons. Some want to promote the image that the workplace is a family. The idea here is that workplace family members love one another and help each other out. (Sorry, did you see my eyes rolling there? We'll discuss the reason why I rolled my eyes in Chapter 3 of the book under "One Big Happy Family"). Another reason would be that they are of the opinion that hierarchy impedes creative growth and a veneer of equal treatment encourages productivity.

Fact of the matter is, our placement in the hierarchy gives us entitlement and power. That ain't equal treatment. That's rank. That's as much damn rank as there is between Gomer Pyle and Sergeant Carter. That ain't Hannibal, Face, Murdock and B.A. Baracus. Hannibal, Face, Murdock and B.A. contribute to the A-Team "horizontally". That means that they do different but equal parts of the work process. Gomer Pyle and Sergeant Carter are in "vertical integration". That means that they do different parts of the work process which are differentiated according to priority, power and value. Sergeant Carter's work obviously has more priority and value than Pyle's. Sergeant Carter accordingly has more power than Pyle.

As I mentioned above, our relative ranks, appointments and positions in the workplace imbue us with different imperatives. So, what are these imperatives?

Management is concerned with getting the maximum output from Staff, while giving them the least possible returns. Least possible, without pushing them to quit, of course. I mean, if they start thinking that the amount of work they put in is not worth the returns they get, they will quit. And by "returns", I mean salary plus perks plus benefits plus bonus plus commission plus whatever ever. Management is not likely to pay a Staffer more than what they think he's worth. If he comes in as a fresh graduate, they'll pay him basic. If he comes in with a Master's degree and work experience they'll pay him slightly more. Why? Because to Management, the applicant with Masters and work experience will be more productive. Will they pay a Staffer extra out of good faith? Will they pay a Staffer extra because he seems earnest? Nope. They'll pay him only as much as they think he's worth. If that Staffer will work for less pay, even better. They'll pay him that.

On the flip side, Staffers are concerned with maximizing their returns and satisfaction while minimizing their effort. "Returns", again, refers to the same thing mentioned in the paragraph above, which is salary plus perks plus benefits plus bonus plus commission plus whatever ever. By "satisfaction" here, I am referring to the whole gamut of emotive aspects of the job, such as being given manageable challenges, being involved in decision-making, having a sense of ownership and having the feeling that one is actually doing meaningful work that one enjoys. Also, we all are concerned with minimizing our effort. "Effort" here refers to the pooled amount of energy we put in to work and work-related tasks. It, of course, includes the amount of work that we put in doing the actual work tasks. We want to perform these tasks quickly, efficiently, and move on to the next. We certainly do not appreciate receiving unclear instructions, causing us to have to redo the work. Ain't that right? It also includes the amount of work that we do as part of a team. We want to work as equally hard as the other fella. We don't want to be the workhorse, doing everything that is required in the team, just to have the other members of our team sit idly by. For the same amount of salary per team member, we'd expect the work to be divided equally. It also includes the effort we need to make in order to work effectively with our colleagues and Bosses. Some colleagues and Bosses are pretty easy to work with. Others, not so. It takes a helluva lot for us to get through to them. Sometimes, they can't understand us. Other times, they just don't want to. Chapters 1 and 2 are devoted to working with such "peachy" colleagues and Bosses. It also includes other auxiliary efforts such as the commute to work. We've all seen the videos of commuter trains in Japan and India where commuters have to be pushed and squeezed into trains during rush hour. We've all also been in traffic jams so long, time seemed to be moving backwards. If we had a choice, wouldn't we want to put in less effort to get to work? A shorter trip, maybe? Or a more comfortable ride, maybe?

The key to our needs at the workplace is balance. The costs (or, "effort" as mentioned in the previous paragraph) associated with working there must not outstrip the benefits (that is, "returns" and "satisfaction"). We don't mind putting in more effort, as long as it brings us more satisfaction and remuneration. But, when we perceive that our returns and satisfaction from the workplace is decreasing, we will take steps to reduce our effort accordingly. For example, when there is a pay cut, or when our suggestions are not taken seriously, we'll put in less effort, so as to maintain the balance. And so the old adage goes, "pay peanuts, get monkeys".

As mentioned earlier, we all bring a little something something to the table at the workplace. We're never exact clones with each other, and because of that, there are plenty of opportunities for misunderstanding, clashes and unhappiness between colleagues. Thomas Hobbes tells us, through his classic work *The Leviathan*, that in order for humans to live (in this case, work) together, they have to sign a "social contract" with each other. This social contract prevents chaos, and without this contract, there will be a "war of all against all". It would become Darwinian, with competitive pressures pushing each individual to care only for his or her own needs, wants and desires. A social contract thus reminds people that they agree to not harm each other but rather to try to work for a mutual good.

Let me address two points here.

Firstly, in the workplace, there is not just a social contract. There is a legal contract between the employee and the legal entity that is the organization. Some of us are bounded by a notice of resignation. We can't leave the organization the next day, but rather, have to serve a period of a month, or two months, or three. Some of us are bounded by a clause of non-competition.

That means we cannot poach our former clients or join a competitor for a pre-determined period of time.

Secondly, this social contract is not always binding at the workplace. The Darwinian Devil does rear its ugly head more often than we think. Of course, in the ideal workplace, everyone does their fair share. As sung in the *LEGO Movie*, "Everything is awesome… everything is cool when you're part of a team". In the ideal workplace, everyone is equally motivated, equally talented and have their eye on a common prize, that is, "the greatest good for the greatest number", to quote John Stuart Mill, Jeremy Bentham and the utilitarian social thinkers. In the ideal workplace, everyone comes in the morning with a smile and leaves in the evening with an even bigger smile. In the ideal workplace, everyone cleans up their own goddamn mess in the goddamn pantry. But this doesn't always happen, does it?

The scenario of the "tragedy of the Commons" in game theory illustrates this very well. The Commons refers to a communal grazing area where English farmers would bring their cows to graze. One could say that every farmer is free to bring his cows whenever he wants, because, hey, no one owns that spot anyway. But think about this. If every uddertrucking farmer brought all his uddertrucking cows to eat the uddertrucking grass every single uddertrucking day, it would be no time at all before the grass is all gone. So there must be a system, or a social contract, following the terms we're using right now, to ensure that the grass is not depleted, so that every farmer can enjoy the free graze until the end of time. Yes, at first every farmer agrees to take turns, but soon after, something will crop up. Farmer Smith has to go to Sussex tomorrow, so he has to bring his cows to graze today. But today is not his turn. It's Farmer Brown's turn. Farmer Brown has come to graze, and gone home. So who's gonna know if Farmer Smith cheats a day, right? So he brings his cows to graze today. What harm could it do, come on?

Pretty soon, every other farmer has an excuse, and the contract is broken like an arrow. And once the social contract is broken, the Commons will turn into a spot where every farmer brings his cows willy nilly on his own time to graze as much as they want, without regard for the other farmers in the area. The grass will eventually not have time to replenish itself naturally, and start to deplete. And the Commons becomes a tragedy. Individual greed, without adherence to the social contract, spoiled the Commons for one and all.

What am I trying to say here? That even with a social contract, life is still pretty much Darwinian.

There is an ecological system that we're a part of. Yup, the workplace is one such ecological system. Our place in the food chain determines the type and quality of resources we get. Simply put, the CEO gets to take a dump in the restroom with the golden taps. Staffers get to share the restroom with the janitor who ate an extra spicy burrito for dinner last night.

There is definitely competition in the workplace. We all know the popular cliche that goes, "There is no "I" in team". Hell, yes, there is. Without the individual putting in effort, the team would not exist. Try to get one individual to contribute to all the tasks in the team, while the rest sit idly by shooting the breeze. Would that individual be happy? Hell, no. When the "I"s come together at the workplace, competition will ensue. Competition in the workplace can take many forms. We compete to get promoted, to get noticed, to get recognized, to get offered the highest profile projects, and so on. Unfortunately, most of us engage in blind competition. With every effort put in, we hope to receive remuneration and satisfaction commensurate with that effort. But that rarely happens, doesn't it? Our organizations never tell us in perfect transparency how we're faring in relation to our objectives, or even in relation to our colleagues. They keeps us in the dark, so that, just like Schrodinger's cat, we are always excelling and not excelling at work at any one time. I have a stinging suspicion that our organizations are taking lessons from Pavlov's dogs too. By keeping us not completely informed, they're conditioning us in an operant manner. That is to say, "If you want this prize, you'll press the right buttons". That's "reinforcement" right there. Press the wrong buttons, and they'll either withhold our treats (negative punishment), or whip us with a switch (positive punishment).

Another point to add about competition is that there aren't two spots for first prize. Or following the phrase popularized by *Highlander*, "There can be only one". This follows the "principle for competitive exclusion" in Darwinian ecology, where two species which attempt to exploit that same set of finite resources cannot coexist, because one will attempt to exclude the other. In the same vein, many organizations have been using the method of "forced ranking", where Management, by definition, must rank staffers according to performance. Staffers cannot all be equally contributive. Staffers cannot all be equally lousy. There can be one who's the Employee of the Month, and then the rest are in second, third, and umpteenth place.

Our survival at the workplace depends quite largely on the returns and satisfaction we're getting from the workplace environment. We will survive if and only if we're getting the resources that we desire. Otherwise, we'd get angsty. We'd get angry. We'd get jaded. We'd fall sick. We'd quit. We might even die on the job, as some people in Japan and Korea have (see recent article in *Japan Today*). Imagine this scenario. We put effort into our jobs. We work hard for 364 days, and on the 365th day, we discover that John Doe in the next cubicle gets the fatter year-end bonus. Did we get the resources that we desire? No. The smaller year-end bonus may get us through the holidays fine and dandy, but we did not get that recognition that we wanted, did we now? Imagine this other scenario. We take up a new job because it gives us time for our family. We may have just had a baby, and having no other help, we need time off to take care of the baby. We discover, soon enough, that our knock-off time gets later and later. We are asked to come in to work even on the weekends. We get paid quite a fair bit for this extra work, but are we getting the resources we desire? Again, no. We need the time, not the money. And if time is not what we're getting from this job, then we're not getting what we want.

We are rational beings. We may not always be logical, but we are certainly rational. By which I mean, we always do mental calculations and look for the best possible circumstance for our own benefit. To our rational minds, our own personal costs from any endeavor should not exceed the benefits. Sure, we may extend a helping hand to a colleague who is in dire need for someone to cover his shift, but we do so because it offers either a return favor, or it makes us feel good that we have done something good for someone. Indeed, this rationality can be either implicit or explicit, and it certainly means that "there is no free lunch". Nothing is unconditional. We always seek to preserve ourselves, our interests, and our existence.

While neoclassical economists refer to this as "Homo economicus", I would prefer to argue along the lines of Herbert Simon, who put forth the idea of "bounded rationality". What this means is that we are all wired to perform cost-benefit calculations so that we don't make wrong decisions, but we're not always able to compute all the figures. For one, "we don't know what we don't know". There is a large sphere of information that we don't even know exists. We know some things. We don't know other things. But there are some other things that, if we were to find out, we'd exclaim, "I never thought I'd live to see this!" For another, we don't always have all the resources to go in search of options indefinitely. We either get bored, or we don't have the time to, or we just lose hope. We are thus "satisficing", to use another of Herbert Simon's terms. Yet another reason is because we could perhaps be just cognitively unable to process such a barrage of information. Of course, it is nice to believe that everyone can understand each other perfectly well, but that's not always the case. Speaking to some people is like speaking to a wall. We just can't get through to them!

Why do we have such different levels of cognition? Well, simply put, different people have different levels of intelligence. Everyone is smart, but some are just smarter than others. Face it. It is a fact of life. This intelligence can be something that we're born with, or something we develop through learning from experience and our own reflections. There are many ways to measure intelligence, but most importantly, intelligence has a strong bearing on cognition.

Another reason why we have different levels of cognition is that not everyone thinks in a clear, concise, logical, critical manner. In philosophy, there are several colorful terms used to describe "logical fallacies", that is to say, flaws in argumentation. Terms such as "red herring", "straw man", "slippery slope", "no true Scotsman" and such are used to describe erroneous ways to present arguments. Yet, these fallacies are not just behavioral. That is to say, we don't choose to make flawed arguments. These fallacies have a cognitive basis. In other words, we make flawed arguments because we are unable to interpret the information that we receive in a clear, concise, critical way. Take a look at racial profiling, as a simple example. Some people were brought up to think ill of persons of other ethnicities. They've been taught to hate because it is part of the culture that they grew up in. Others just fall backwards into racial profiling through their own cognitive limitations. It doesn't take much for the human brain to profile and generalize. Just a few chance encounters of persons of certain ethnicities exhibiting certain undesirable behaviors, and the brain will conclude, "Oh, so all the people of this certain ethnicity behave in this way, innit?" Once the brain cognitively interprets this as such, our behaviors follow suit. That's when we start to present "hasty generalizations".

So far, we've established that despite there being a legal and social contract, the workplace still has a "war of all against all". But are colleagues always engaged in battle all the time? No. The physical action of engaging in war is referred to as "hot war" by militarists. This is when you send in the troops and engage in bloody battle until one of the armies is completely annihilated or surrenders. No, it isn't always hot war at the workplace. At times, it might be a cold war, where parties involved at the workplace are building defenses and alliances in preparation for any future incidence of hot war. At other times it might be a siege, where parties involved in the workplace are just waiting to tire the other fellow out so that he surrenders. At other times, it might be espionage, where parties involved in the workplace are gathering information on each other so that this information might be used against them when the time comes. Or it could be any other form of struggle, which requires one to be on one's defense, and to keep in mind some strategies for offense. That's what I mean by "war".

The workplace war is comprised of the defensive and offensive strategies one adopts in one's rational capacity for self-preservation at the workplace. We could say that this rational capacity for self-preservation is an extension of the good ol' "fight or flight" response built into our basal instincts. We rationalize by calculating our costs and benefits whenever we are faced with people, events and tasks. When we're given a new project to work on, we calculate how much benefit we're going to get from it. When we encounter an incompetent colleague, we calculate how much of this colleague's work we're going to have to pick up. When a new Boss comes into our workplace, we wonder how much change we'd have to make to adapt to his style of working. We don't like change. Change is costly. We'd like to change only when it suits us. Change from within is always welcome. Change from without is always blech.

Our rationalization, however, is almost wholly dependent on our cognitive capacities. We calculate costs and benefits according to what we perceive to be costly and beneficial to us respectively. As they say, "one man's trash is another man's treasure". What we perceive to be beneficial, another person may perceive to be costly, and vice versa. Some of us might think that having to bring work home is not a happy thought. It costs us precious time which could be better spent with our families. Some might just feel the opposite. Bringing work home is a welcome thought, because it means more time for socializing at the office! Equally as important, though, is that because of our "bounded rationalities", we are unable to correctly identify costs and benefits. This is because we just cannot recognize them as costs and benefits. Maybe it's because we've never encountered them before. Maybe it's because we just didn't look hard enough and didn't notice them. Some of us, for example, who have experienced a restructuring exercise in the workplace before, might say, "Uh-oh, another change of structure. Wonder how bad this will turn out. Wonder who will get canned." Others among us, who have never experienced a restructuring exercise before, would not even recognize the impact it might have on us. We might take it lightly and think that it's not even a question. Cognition and rationality will be brought up time and again throughout this book. They will be two of the guiding beacons to get us through all our discussions in this book.

Yet, we cannot discount the importance of emotion. As I always say, you can always teach a person how to think, but you can never tell a person what to feel. As much as we try to rationalize at the workplace, we can't help but surrender to our emotions sometimes. We might recognize the benefits of being chummy with the Boss, for example, but we just cannot bring ourselves to do it. We might recognize the potential danger of posting nasty remarks about colleagues on Facebook, but we just cannot help but vent it out. Our emotions are often tied to our cognitions, as well. When we encounter something at the workplace that we cannot understand, or just cannot possibly agree with, or something that causes us significant dissatisfaction or something that runs very contrary to our expectations (known as "cognitive dissonance"), we get emotionally affected by it. Some of us get angry at those things. Some of us get jaded, and just go along with the flow. Some of us eventually convince ourselves to understand. But most of us just get drained. It saps our energy to have to carry such a heavy cognitive load. This phenomenon is known to some as "psychic vampirism", that is, things, people and events that just simply suck the energy out of us, leaving us drained and tired.

And… I suspect some of you are already tired out by this point. You're already thinking, "Oh that's too much for me. I don't want to think ill of my colleagues. I just want to do my job, that's all." No worries, the section of "The Non-Competitive Ones" in Chapter 1 is just for you. For now, I would say that it would be easy enough to refrain from any and all competition, that is, if all your colleagues agreed to do so as well. But the nature of life in the workplace is that almost all of us are trying to obtain a similar set of resources, such that our costs do not outstrip our benefits. In that process of obtaining resources, we are more likely than not to clash with one another. This will be covered under the section of "Group Preservation" in Chapter 2. In one episode of the sitcom *Scrubs*, Dr Bob Kelso proclaims that "people are bastard-coated bastards with bastard filling". Well, I wouldn't be so quick to profess such a large generalization of human behavior, but I will say this: People will always seek to preserve themselves, and if competition is what it takes, then compete they shall. I'm not saying it's bad. I'm not saying it's good. I'm saying that's just how it is. We're all wired to think and act in that way. And the faster we learn to manage our own survival at the workplace, the better it is for each and every one of us. Yes, this is one thing that we all agree on. Survival. To paraphrase from Guns N' Roses, everything will be roses when we hold on to our guns.

"Can I not just do my best, and everything will work out?", I hear some of you ask. We have all been taught since young that as long as we put in effort into everything we do, we can achieve anything. "Good things happen to good people", we've always been told. Yes, that system works perfectly fine, if we assume that everything, every person, every animal, every machine, every event has a place and has a use in life. But they don't. That system would also work perfectly fine if we assume that our very merits will get us the recognition we deserve. Indeed, almost every organization that I know has such meritocratic policies in place, and procedures to recognize merit. It's a noble intention. But guess what? As always, other things get in the way. Our merits, as it turns out, don't get us recognized as easily as we'd like. Some of these obstacles have been built into the organizational structure. An example of this is the vacancy chains of promotion. In the simplest possible terms, no one can get promoted until someone above them retires or croaks. And the situation is exacerbated when the organization decides to parachute someone from the outside to fill a vacancy. The employees who are next in line for promotion cannot get promoted because that someone from the outside is deemed to be a better replacement for the person who has retired or croaked. Note that when the organization does this, it does it for the sake of meritocracy. The organization may think that the existing employees may not have the right skills and knowledge yet to be promoted. Or it may think that there is someone from the outside who has better skills and knowledge to fill the gap. Noble intentions. Still, the consequences are borne by us common employees. No matter how our organizations try to justify it, our merits are nonetheless not recognized. We still lose.

Some of these obstacles are more social, and less structural in nature. Glass ceilings, for example. Glass ceilings exist when our social identities are deemed to be limiting to our career progress. Historically, women, ethnic minorities and persons of alternative sexuality have been deemed to be less worthy of promotion to higher ranks in organizations, causing them to stagnate after they have reached a certain level. Too many examples of this exist to cite. As the lead singer of Steel Dragon said in the movie *Rock Star*, "It's because I'm gay isn't it?" Aside from gender, ethnic and sexual minorities, employees with divergent ideas and divergent experiences can also face such resistance to progress in organizations. Their lack of perfect fit with the "mainstream" ideas and experience within such organizations invite various degrees of resistance from colleagues and Management alike, ranging from labels of "primary deviance" imposed on them to outright ridicule to poor performance evaluations (more can be read of "primary deviance" in Lemert's seminal article).

Yet other obstacles exist in the cognitive capacities of Managers and fellow colleagues alike. We've all heard of the famous thought experiment: "When a tree falls in a lonely forest, and no animal is nearby to hear it, does it make a sound?" (see the book by Mann and Twiss dated 1910). Extend that to the workplace: "When work is done in a lonely cubicle, and no colleague or Manager is nearby to notice it, does it still count?" Humans tend to notice things which are louder, bigger, gaudier and have a larger, more immediate impact on their lives. Here's an example. Consider these three statements:

Statement 1: We are all going to die someday…

Statement 2: I think someone's out to kill you.

Statement 3: There's a big guy with a Jason mask and a chainsaw headed your way right now!

Which statement made most impact? The third one, of course. Same thing happens at the workplace. The tasks which are louder, bigger, gaudier and have more immediate impact get noticed more. Some of us do jobs which are best described as "thankless". The work that some of us do are treated as hygiene factors at the workplace. If it doesn't get done, we get rapped. If it gets done, no one notices. Whether it gets done well enough, or gets done supercalifragilisticexpialidociously well, meh, no one gives a hoot.

Another cognitive obstacle is the "halo effect", or its opposite, the "horns effect". In simple terms, employees who have been doing laudable work, are rated more leniently for future work. Employees who have been judged as being poor performers will be rated more harshly for future work. In light of these cognitive biases, structural obstacles and social resistance, can we truly rely on our work to speak for itself?

Bottom line is, no, we cannot just put our heads down and do our best at work and everything will work itself out. Our working survival depends on the conflation of three factors: colleagues, Bosses and organizational theatrics. The employees who do best in organizations are the people who fit in well with the colleagues of their level, have a mutual understanding with their Bosses, and are able to play along with the organizational theatrics.

So, why are some people able to work in a job for decades, while others change jobs every couple o' years? Is it just them? Are those who are able to stay more competent than those who don't last? No. It has nothing to do with the individual employee. It has everything to do with the fit between that employee, on one hand, and his colleagues, his Bosses and the organizational theatrics on the other. You see, people change, times change, policies change, core businesses change, basically everything changes. Nothing really stays the same. Nothing lasts forever, not even cold November rain. According to ecologists, there are two general kinds of change, namely, fine-grained and coarse-grained changes. Fine-grained changes are characterized by small changes over long periods of time. Evolution, for example, is a fine-grained change. No one notices the minute adaptations that organisms make in response to the environment until a couple of thousand years after, when one discovers that an organism looks noticeably different from its predecessors. Who would have thought the gargantuan ornithiscian dinosaurs 230 million years ago would eventually become the cute little birdies chirping on our window sills today? Natural disasters, for example, is a coarse-grained change. In a matter of minutes, a tsunami can cause a severe flood, a volcanic eruption can cause a wipeout of land-based animals and an earthquake can swallow everything in its path whole. Needless to say, fine-grained changes are easier to adapt to, rather than coarse-grained changes.

In the organizational setting, a fine-grained change might be, for example, changes to procedure over time based on feedback from employees. A coarse-grained change might be, for example, mass firings and new hirings brought about by the entry of a new CEO, who is hell bent on "cleaning out the closet". In any red-blooded organization, colleagues will come and go. Bosses will come and go. Both colleagues and Bosses will change their attitudes and personas, even if they do stay (this will be explained further in Chapter 2 under "Caveat Lector"). And organizations will adopt new and different theatrics depending on the spirit of the times. During the *Mad Men* days, it was acceptable for men to assume the superior position in organizations. Accordingly, they felt the need to adopt theatrics that show off their superiority vis-a-vis women. Today, the mainstream is different. It is hip to show some semblance of social responsibility, to offset the negative externalities brought about by corporate enterprise. The theatrics today will reflect this, and companies will adopt policies that show off their corporate social responsibilities.

So again, why are some people able to work in a job for decades, while others change jobs every couple o' years? People who stay in the same company for decades are able to do so because they are able to adapt to changes in the organization over that long period of time. And more likely than not, those organizations tend to feature more fine-grained changes rather than coarse-grained changes, because, as mentioned earlier, fine-grained changes are easier to adapt to rather than coarse-grained changes. The reverse is true for people who change jobs every few years. They are less able to adapt to changes in the organization, and it is more likely than not that those organizations tend to feature coarse-grained changes rather than fine-grained changes, causing disruption to the survival of their employees and consequent resignations.

Don't worry. It's not you. It's the workplace war. War makes monsters of us all.

# CHAPTER 1: HOW TO SURVIVE INCOMPETENT COLLEAGUES

We've all been there before. Every time we start a new job, we get introduced around the office and shake hands with everyone all around. Everyone seems equal at that point. One hand feels just the same as another. Sure, we can make fleeting judgments about some of them. We might think this fellow's handshake is a little too firm, or this other colleague is pretty good looking, but we all know these fleeting judgments will soon change. By the time we get down to work, we'll start forming other judgments instead. To be fair, not all colleagues are incompetent. We all are irked by incompetent colleagues, aren't we? But there are many other types of colleagues too. In this chapter, we will be looking at various types of colleagues, how to maneuver around them, and some things you need to know about declaring war and making alliances.

## TYPES OF COLLEAGUES

Let's take a look at some archetypal colleagues here. You would probably recognize most of these, having encountered them in your working lives. We'll be discussing The Gossipmonger, whose penchant for dramatizing events at work never ceases to astound, The Whisperer, who has his lips permanently sutured to Management's ears, The Keyboard Warrior, the most macho soul to ever grace Planet Email, The Mouse, who tread lightly on their own shadows and The Captains of Incompetence, whose deadweight we have to carry around like a sack of potatoes.

## THE GOSSIPMONGER

Gossipmongers are colleagues who spend hours dramatizing social relationships at work. They take in a fact, add salt, pepper and preservatives, then churn it out into a TV dinner, and sell it to other colleagues around. They love stories about others, and will not shy away from a good gossip. Why do they love to gossip so much? Well, one theory has it that they're too free. As far as this theory goes, if their time were to be filled up with meaningful work, they wouldn't gossip as much. There is some truth to this, although I wouldn't agree with it completely. Gossipmongers will always find time for gossip, even if it means cutting corners and scrimping on the time allocated for work. Why? Because they define gossip as being an integral resource at work. And as all ecological beings do, they seek to maximize the gathering of this resource.

And what about the part whereby they process the gossip? Ah, that's where their own existential self-preservation comes into being. By processing the information in the way they choose, they're taking control of the resource, and by taking control, they're making it a part of their existential selves. In *Freakanomics*, we learnt that we often fear what we cannot control, and this is why we fear airplane crashes and terrorist hijacks more than road accidents. We know that there is a higher probability that we might meet our tragic end in a road accident than an airplane crash, but we are existentially assured that we won't meet with a road accident because we're driving and we're in control. "Not if I can help it", we say.

So, how do we maneuver around Gossipmongers? Gossipmongers are annoying, I must agree. They're like flies buzzing around in Australia in summertime. Stand still for one brief moment, and one will land on your nose or fly into your ear. There are two ways to deal with Gossipmongers.

One way is to starve them of the very resource they desire. Gossip. That's right. Don't give them any. Like crackheads though, they'll come looking for it. They'll either come looking for it during tea breaks or lunch, or they'll accost us while we're alone in the pantry. Pay attention to their patterns. Avoid the time they usually go to lunch, so that they have no chance of asking us to join them. Excuse ourselves five minutes before lunchtime to "make a call" or "visit the little boy's room" and disappear from their sight. Pay attention to their whereabouts. They will be looking for opportunities to get us alone, so don't give them that opportunity. Treat them like that fella with the squeegee we want to avoid at the traffic light. Treat them like that crazy drunk guy who keeps wanting to talk to us at the local liquor store. Slip away.

Another way is to bait them with a long trail of false gossip that would eventually turn really ridiculous, or would put their feet in their mouths. The first gossip we offer them will be something general. Like "I went to work this morning and I saw an empty bottle in the parking lot". The next gossip we give them should extend that tale, but also go in the direction of becoming extremely ridiculous. Keep telling them gossip after gossip, until they realize that they're being played. If they don't realize it yet, carry on the tale, and add stupider and stupider elements to it. Eventually, they'll realize they're being made a fool of, and they'll slink away like a snake defeated. The resource they thought they were getting, turns out to be a dud. They thought they were going to get the sweet nectar of peaches, yet all they got was a plastic table decorative fruit.

Yet another way is to completely look through them. That is, pretend that they're not even there at all. They hate that. Gossipmongers love attention, and when it is not given to them, they'll get that monkey on their backs. A Gossipmonger will flaunt his new haircut, his new shirt, his new smartphone. He'll parade around the office like it was Mardi Gras. Pretend not to notice. He'll most likely step up his efforts to get our attention. Keep on pretending. If he is desperate enough, he'll make a direct line to us and ask us in no uncertain terms, "How's my haircut?" Reply, in uncertain terms, "Huh? Oh, I didn't notice. It's nice." Any further attempts on their part to make small talk should be blocked. Try to end any conversations they initiate within two minutes.

## THE WHISPERER

Whisperers are Staffers who are close to Managers. They either are on the way to Management positions, or they could be golf buddies with a certain Manager, or they could even be sleeping with another Manager. Whatever it might be, Whisperers whisper. They whisper tiny little bits of information to Management that they gather around the office. Kind of like what Caesar Milan does to dogs and Jackson Galaxy does to cats, I suppose? They are keen observers, and they also trade information with each other. The scariest thing about the Whisperers is not that they whisper, but that their whispers actually are paid attention to by Management. This will be covered in Chapter 2 under "Manager-Staffer Alliances".

But why do Whisperers whisper? It might surprise you to know that Whisperers do so for a variety of reasons. One reason might be that they are explicitly trying to curry the favor of Management. We all know the familiar cartoon sycophant who says "Yes, Boss" to everything the villain says, while the villain gleefully strokes his cat and says, "Excellent, excellent!" Another reason might be that they have formed the opinion that it is in their job scope or duty to report anything that isn't right. These Whisperers hold a moral compass and act a little bit like Boy Scouts, but fact of the matter is, they see that doing the right thing is an obligation of theirs. They define it as their existential characteristic. By not doing the right thing, they will feel uneasy, and unfulfilled, just like as if someone is threatening their existential selves. But as we all know, the "right" thing is as slippery as unagi to define. Indeed, these Whisperers define what is right, according to what they think it should be. This often is the result of their moral upbringing, but could also be due to idiosyncratic preference. "Doing the right thing" is thus one of the valued resources, the way Whisperers reckon.

Tread carefully among these. They are loaded guns. One way you can maneuver around them is to ally with them. This will be covered under the section "Making Alliances" below. Allying with a Whisperer is good because Whisperers are in an advantageous position in the food chain. They eat scraps from the Master's table, but these scraps likely taste way better than the swill the rest of us have. Whisperers also possess resources that we can put to good use, such as knowledge on performance appraisals, access to key projects, and the like.

If we can't ally with them, treat them at arms-length. Treat them as we would Management. Greet them formally, and if we can, refer to them by rank and surname. When they try to engage us in conversation, end that conversation as quickly as possible. Keep all channels of communication formal. That way, neither Whisperers nor Management can claim that we're rude or insubordinate.

Are we actually thinking rationally here? We sure are. We want to maximize the effort we spend doing actual work, and minimize the uncertainty of work politics. By allying with the Whisperers, we are maximizing certainty. We are buying favors from them, so that we get an advantage point. By not engaging with Whisperers, we are minimizing uncertainty. We are reducing our chances of getting sliced for non-task-related matters. These non-task-related matters can hit us like a ton of bricks when we least expect it. We don't want our performance appraisals to contain prejudicial phrases such as "demonstrated insubordination" or "presented himself in a caustic manner" or "did not appeal much to the rest of the office", do we?

## THE KEYBOARD WARRIOR

Keyboard Warriors are colleagues whose persona appears as a towering Atilla the Hun-like character, but only over email. For added effect, they'll also keep Management in the cc list of any email they send. And for even more additional effect, they'll cc anyone else who they think needs to know about the contents of that email. Quite usually, they won't be Atilla the Hun in real life. They might be meek, or they might be actually nice, or perhaps even a quiet stammering sort. But over email, watch out. They can make sailors blush.

Why do these Keyboard Warriors exist? Oftentimes, Keyboard Warriors hide behind the less-personal nature of email. Many years ago, organizational psychologists such as Joseph Champoux had suggested that Managers should not have conversations with Staffers behind desks. They said that desks provide a sort of wall from behind which Managers can safely fire orders and chastise staffers. To have a more candid, open conversation, they said, have such conversations on a couch-and-armchair setting. And sit not opposite each other, but side by side. In the digital age, email has become the new "desk". It has become the new convenient way to safely "speak" to colleagues without actually speaking to them. The phenomenon of "management by email" is often a very convenient way of assuming Managerial duties, where Managers simply shoot orders and ask for deliverables through email. But as we shall find out later, Management's ammunition can be our ammunition too. We too, can use email to our advantage. These will be covered under the sections of "The Simulator" and "Fighting Capabilities" in the next chapter.

So, are Keyboard Warriors acting like rational beings? They certainly are. They have calculated the opportunity costs of communicating in other ways, and they personally feel that there is less to lose with communicating with strong words over email, rather than communicating with strong words through other channels such as face-to-face or over the office telephone. What is there to lose, we might think? It's just about work, anyway, right? That's us. Remember that different people have different levels of cognition. Keyboard Warriors understand work communication differently. Keyboard Warriors may not be quite able to hold a real-time conversation and need a delayed reaction time. Hence, they turn to email. Keyboard Warriors may not be able to perform under the pressure of a verbal confrontation. Hence, they turn to email. Keyboard Warriors may not want to make someone feel bad, or at least be in the presence of someone who they made feel bad. This is the reason why some husbands ask for a divorce from their wives over phone text (I'm not kidding. Refer to the article in *Emirates 24/7*). They just want to get it over and done with, and not face whatever is they might face should they ask for a divorce face-to-face. Also the reason why there are several executioners during a firing squad. No executioner wants to know that he was one who put the fatal bullet into the prisoner (see US Army Manual from 1947).

So, how do we maneuver around Keyboard Warriors? Treat them like fish, and take them out of water. Takes a little bit of sadism on our part, but hey, we do what we have to, don't we? Since Keyboard Warriors rule email-land, we should not engage them in battle over email. They know that terrain better than we do. They are fearless berserkers in that terrain. To engage them on that terrain, we'd need to spend a lot of time knowing the topography of that terrain. We must ensure that we have enough resources to capture that entire terrain. Now, military logic dictates that such an enterprise would be quite difficult. A much easier way would be to bring Keyboard Warriors out into a terrain where they are uncomfortable, and thus can't quite react as explosively as they would over email. What other terrains can there be? Plenty. Lunch. Tea. Staff meetings. Pantry. Or easier still, just go over to their cubicles. On those grounds, it's fair game. We can get them to agree to take on our work. We can get them to agree to finish up their part of the project. They will be like a fish out of water, trying to evade us in a terrain they are unfamiliar with. And always make mention of their preferred terrain while they're on ours. Say something like, "OK, nice chat. So we've agreed on some things haven't we? Now would you mind if I put all this in writing? All you have to do is to reply to the email I am going to send you with a "received" or "noted"."

## THE MOUSE

Scottish poet Robert Burns, in 1785, said, "The best-laid schemes o' mice an' men gang aft agley (often go awry)". As much as we try to make plans to keep our lives in order, unexpected things happen, leaving us with grief and pain. The Mouse is one type of colleague who is extra careful that this does not happen to them.

In fact, Mice live within a cocoon of fear at the workplace. They keep that cocoon for any circumstance that might even tangentially involve workplace matters, such as office parties, the bar that colleagues go to, or even their own neighborhoods, if their other colleagues were to live there too. They're really really really concerned what others think of them, and therefore try to put their best face forward all the time. Mice often think very carefully about the words they use with others. They spend a lot of time crafting emails with such sweet overtones so as to make it damn near impossible for the recipients of said emails to mistake their nice intentions. Synonyms are more than synonyms to Mice. They see each and every word imbued with such powerful connotations that using the wrong word could mean a penalty worse than death. It's not just about political correctness. Oh, it's way more than that. Political correctness has the intention of offering fairness to persons who are prone to disadvantage by referring to them using terms which do not exaggerate this disadvantage. Political correctness is about those prone to disadvantage. Mice being nice, on the other hand, is not about others. Mice want to be nice for their own benefit.

Mice would see a world of difference between, for example, "I need your help", "I would like your help" and "I want your help". Mice would see a world of difference between, for example, "This is wrong" and "This is inaccurate".

Stop the beat. Up for a more ludicrous example? One of my clients informed me that his colleague disapproved one of the songs he chose for a company event. I immediately formed the image in my mind that that song had explicit lyrics and was thus inappropriate for airplay. Maybe it was a Snoop Dogg song. Or maybe it was a Slipknot song. Nope. How wrong I was. It was the song "Read 'em John". "Read 'em John" is a song from the slavery era in South Carolina and Georgia. This type of "ring shout" song is characterized by call-and-response singing, clapping and stomping the floor. To the slaves, this was a very powerful song. This song spoke about a certain person, John, who was able to read. The ability to read was seen by the slaves as a vehicle for emancipation. So, wait. What was wrong with the song again? According to my client's colleague, that song was inappropriate because it was from the slavery era. That colleague was afraid that the participants at that company event would get offended because they might develop the impression that my client was calling them "slaves" by playing that song.

I'll let that stupidity sit and stew for a bit. I'll wait while you catch your breath.

So, why do Mice live in fear of what others think about them? They invest a lot in their nice-guy image. They define their existential selves as the one who everybody likes. More Raymond less Chris. (Did anyone get that? I was pitting *Everybody Loves Raymond* against *Everybody Hates Chris*). They do not mind investing so much cognitive effort in choosing the right words, no matter how unnecessary it looks to the rest of us. Mice are the embodiment of the Japanese phrase "the nail that sticks out gets hammered down". They don't want to be that nail, no sirree bob.

Mice aren't the jocks who go at it on the basketball court. They don't sweat. They don't push other players around. They don't curse at each other. They don't smack each other on the asses after a good play. They sit in the bleachers and cheer. They're happy to do that and only that.

I'm not sure we'd need to maneuver around Mice at all. They mean well, but their lack of cajones might annoy some of us bolder ones from time to time. If you ask me, I'd say just keep them in their lab cages. They won't try to take over the world like Pinky and the Brain would.

And finally we get to the namesakes of this chapter...

## THE CAPTAINS OF INCOMPETENCE

Captains of Incompetence actually refer to a group of ragtag individuals. They are far from being a monolithic group. We just refer to the whole lot of them as "incompetent" because they make us carry their deadweight around. Some colleagues are incompetent because they just don't have the skillset to carry the workload like the rest of us. We might be inclined to call these "The Fumb Ducks" for lack of a more flattering term. For lack of training or experience, these colleagues do less than the rest of us because they just can't do any more than that. Human resource practitioners such as Robert Mathis et al suggest that such employees who are unable to perform to expectation should be redeployed and redesignated to areas of the organization where they could contribute better than in their current position. Retraining could also be a viable option. However, in reality, this hardly happens. Why? To Management, there are a lot of costs involved in redeployment, redesignation and retraining. There are, of course, the financial costs of sending someone to training and loss of productivity during that period. There also transaction costs involved in managing such a transfer. Time has to be taken to explain to the Staffer why he has to be redeployed, redesignated and retrained. Effort has to be made to ensure that there is no stigma associated with that Staffer's transfer (more on "transaction costs" under "Declaration of War" below). To Management, these costs far outstrip the benefits of redeployment, redesignation and retraining. As such, Management cognitively prefers to see productivity at the team level, instead of at the individual level. In other words, Management is quite happy for more competent Staffers to pick up the slack for the Fumb Ducks, so that the overall level of productivity of the team is maintained. Instead of ensuring that every single Staffer contributes equally to productivity, it costs less for Management to use the competent Staffers as "slack resources" to compensate for the lower productivity of the Fumb

Ducks. This will be revisited under "The Work Process" in Chapter 3.

Then there are those who don't want to do any more than they should. They're happy for us to take on their workload because, hey, they're getting the same pay as we are, for doing a fraction of the work. We might be inclined to refer to these as the "The Dazy Logs", for lack of a more flattering term. Rational, they are, for they actually calculate the monetary value of their effort and adjust their willingness to work accordingly. Some Dazy Logs get treated in the same way as Fumb Ducks above. They are left alone because Management cognitively perceives productivity to occur at the team level, instead of at the individual level. Some Dazy Logs are more akin to the Actors, who will be discussed next. They don't explicitly show their laziness. They only do as much as they need to, and don't bother with the other additional work that needs to be done. They manage the amount of effort they put into the work process so that their work equation remains balanced on the side of benefits.

And then there are those who act like they're putting in effort but are actually not putting in any. These types can play their part so well that they're just one step away from an Academy Award for Best Actor in the Workplace. Well, two can play at that game. By the time you're through with this book, you will be able to put on an act too, if you so desire. You will know how to, but you don't necessarily have to put that skill to use. Now that's power.

So, wait, how do these "Actors" put in effort while not putting in any? They use the feign of cosmetics. They will package their responses, work effort and deliverables in pretty packages with bows on top, but the contents are not exactly good effort. How? One of the things they might do is to tell Management what Management wants to hear. If Management wants to hear a witty tagline, that's what Actors will focus on… rather than the actual work. If Management wants to hear praises for their leadership, that's what Actors will focus on… rather than the actual work. If Management wants to hear about team harmony, that's what Actors will focus on… rather than the actual work. The Actor's role fits very well into Chapter 3 of this book, which focuses on workplace theatrics. But what about the actual work? Who's doing that? Not the Actors for sure! The Actors will find ways to get someone else to do the actual work for them. They'll either bully some poor sod who can't stand up for himself (we refer to these as The Doormats scantily below), or cajole some other well-intentioned colleague to do the work for them.

In the final analysis, Captains of Incompetence are acting rationally. They are actually quite aware of their inadequacies (such as lack of skill, lack of motivation or lack of desire) and are making up for it by minimizing their effort. For them, difference between the effort spent performing tasks and the actual measurable output of that effort results in their "opportunity cost".

A person who puts in a ton of effort and produces a small iota of productivity has a high opportunity cost. With that time and energy spent, one could have done other tasks. A person who puts in a little bit of effort but produces a lot has a low opportunity cost. A low opportunity cost is good… it means that little effort has been wasted in performing tasks. That's what we're all gunning for, actually aren't we? Look, come on, if we come in to the office at 0900 hours, make three calls to clients and sell a million dollars' worth of goods, would that not be a yippee-ki-yay moment? Hell, I'd spend the rest of the day with my feet on the desk if that were to happen to me! And for Captains of Incompetence, since they know they can't (or won't) up their productivity, they'd rather just reduce the amount of effort they put in so that they won't have a high opportunity cost. The math adds up.

Captains of Incompetence are by far the hardest to maneuver around. Why do I say that? Because Captains of Incompetence, unfortunately, are often protected by Management. But then again, we all already know that, don't we? At least that's how it looks like more often than we care for. But let me clarify though. It's not that Management and Captains of Incompetence are natural allies, you see (this will be covered in Chapter 2 under "Manager-Staffer Alliances"). But there are two main reasons why Captains of Incompetence seem to always be on the good side of Management.

Firstly, Captains of Incompetence often double up their efforts when Management is watching. They will conspicuously demonstrate their performance in the language that Management understands. Imagine a company roadshow, where a Captain of Incompetence is on duty together with some other colleagues. While the other colleagues are setting up the booth, the Captain of Incompetence is doing something completely unhelpful, like picking his nose. While the other colleagues are soliciting interest from the general public, the Captain of Incompetence is taking a break. As soon as there are visitors to the booth, the Captain of Incompetence gets to work. He'll whip out his camera phone and start snapping photos, which he will then quickly send to everyone's email, including Management. Certainly looks productive to Management, doesn't it?

Secondly, organizations have rules. Rules pile on top of rules. Once set, rules are difficult to remove. Captains of Incompetence have mastered the knack of hiding behind these rules, in tiny little corners where they just slip under the organizational radar. By putting in just enough effort, Captains of Incompetence are able to maintain a substantial level of subsistence in the organization in the eyes of Management. In our eyes, they're not pulling their weight, but hey, in Management's eyes, Captains of Incompetence are doing a-ok. This will be revisited under the section of "The Work Process" in Chapter 3.

Thirdly, some Captains of Incompetence actually have a "symbiotic relationship" with certain Managers. In other words, certain Managers have a use for certain Captains of Incompetence, and reciprocally, certain Captains of Incompetence have a use for certain Managers. What we see in Captains of Incompetence may not be what Managers cognitively see, you know. We see a Captain of Incompetence whose slack we have to pick up. Managers see another side they can use. They might see a potential supporter for their cause, or they might see a yes-man who they can get to do their bidding.

Fourthly, we can't discount the "messiah complex" on the part of Managers. The "messiah complex" is a state of mind where a person thinks of himself as a savior, and is able to change another person for the better. The messiah complex often affects persons who are given the status of a leader, but it is not purely altruistic. The messiah complex can be self-serving as well. By putting hope into a Staffer, a Manager with a messiah complex hopes that the Staffer can turn into an exemplary employee, and with that, the Manager will be recognized as the person who turned the Staffer around. The recognition as someone who has helped another person change appeals to the Manager, because it gives him street cred among his fellow Managers.

## CAVEAT LECTOR

A caveat must be preached here. I have chosen to conceptualize colleagues here as "archetypes", following Plato, rather than Weber's "ideal types" or Tonnies's "normal types". This is because, similar to Plato, I see the archetypes of colleagues as being larger-than-life, which can serve as models for real-life imitation. Also, being set in the workplace, the roles these colleagues play look a lot to me like the roles played by actors on a stage (more on the theatrical aspects of the workplace later below in Chapter 3). One further point I would like to make about the caveat I am preaching here is that categorization is never complete. A very good example of categorization that was never complete is the categorization of "races" by colonial powers. In 1775, Johann Friedrich Blumenbach proposed five major divisions: the Caucasoid race, Mongoloid race, Ethiopian race (later termed the Negroid race), American Indian race, and Malayan race. Yet, in India, the British were struggling with classifying the Indians as belonging to Caucasoid, Mongoloid or Negroid, with the ones providing the greatest challenge being the Dravidian peoples. They were sometimes classified as Caucasoid, sometimes as Negroid, and sometimes as their own "Homo Dravida" race. (Refer to the books by Graves and Robb for accounts on the difficulty of classifying people into races.)

These archetypes are neither exhaustive nor mutually exclusive. There are other types of colleagues too, who I have either chosen to exclude because their effects on our working lives are not quite as significant as the ones I mentioned above. Other types of colleagues, include, for example, Janus-faced colleagues who pretend to be sincere but are gearing up to stick a knife into our backs. They mask up before coming to work, and are quite dangerous. Common, isn't it? In fact, I might even say that every colleague has the potential to turn in a Janus. Either they're dormant Januses, or their Janusity was forced by circumstance.

Januses are so common and iconic in the workplace that I've chosen to feature them on the front cover of this very book. They dress just like any of us, they carry workbags just like any of us, but they are so commonplace that they're faceless. Anyone in the workplace can wear that Janus face.

Some Januses start off nice, but eventually see benefit in sticking a knife in our backs, perhaps to gain favor with Management. Other Januses just saw a great opportunity to bring us down, and went for the jugular. Yet other colleagues were quite certain they won't turn into Januses, but when they feel that it is either us or them, they'd rather betray us than face negative consequences themselves. The "prisoner's dilemma" in game theory and in police investigative techniques acknowledge this. If a criminal duo is caught and both criminals are isolated, chances are, each will betray the other and claim that it was the other person's idea. Each criminal is trying to get the least possible sentence for himself, at the expense of the other member. If both were to remain silent and not rat the other out, there will be a chance that they could either both go scot free, or both get sentenced for the crime they committed. Not wanting to take that chance, though, each member will want to secure his own freedom at the expense of the other, and will as such claim it was the other guy's idea and that he was just going along with it.

Then there are the Doormats. They get stepped on by Management and nasty colleagues because they accept tasks way too easily. They don't argue, they just accept. They either fear confrontation, or they fear the reprisal or they're just too damn jaded to fight back. Again, quite a common archetype. We look upon them in pity, but what can we do? They can't bring themselves to be more selective in accepting tasks.

These archetypes are also not mutually exclusive. Not every

colleague is just a Whisperer or a Gossipmonger or a Mouse. A passive-aggressive colleague might be a Gossipmonger-Mouse. Another might be a Keyboard Warrior-Whisperer, who sends chastising emails to us, while keeping Management in the bcc list. Every sort of permutation is possible. A permutated colleague, such as a Captain of Incompetence-Gossipmonger could also be more Captain of Incompetence, less Gossipmonger. Of course then there are the unique snowflakes and mucking funkys who are special blends of the various archetypes above. Archetypes, as they are intended to, represent convenient models of behavior that we can latch our cognitions to, but in real life, they're not necessarily as fixed as this. As semioticians like Charles Sanders Piece argue, the human brain needs to categorize the various things encountered in life in order to understand and retain information. Simple example: the rainbow. Rainbows are actually made up of a continuum of colors as a result of refracted light. Yet, we reduce all these colors to just ROYGBIV (red, orange, yellow, green, blue, indigo and violet). The red in one rainbow may very well look different from the red in another rainbow, but we denote both as red anyway. And what about the colors in between red and orange? Is there a discrete separation between the seven layers? No. Each layer blends into another. We don't account for the variety of blended colors though, because the human brain finds it very difficult to understand and remember continua.

## DECLARATION OF WAR

Ok, so we've all heard this before. Workmates are family. Family members help each other. Family members work towards a common good. Family members don't judge each other. The team, the team, the team. Yadda friggin' yadda.

Fact of the matter is, the workplace is not a family unit. Management wants you to believe it is a family unit because it helps them achieve a level of cohesion. And that level of cohesion could help them realize a higher level of productivity. Which makes them look good.

The workplace is a competitive arena. And as competitive arenas go, one could compete like old folks playing bingo, or one could compete like wildebeests on the plains of South Africa. What I'm saying is that the workplace could turn into a war zone at any given moment. There are colleagues who will conduct espionage and collect intelligence stealthily over a few years. There will also be colleagues who will declare war at the drop of a hat. Believe it or not, there are such brazen people with balls of brass who will point a finger at you in public and claim that you have committed a misdeed.

Truth be told, Staffers do not need to have a public declaration of war in order to launch an offensive. As will be discussed in the section of "Fighting Capabilities" in Chapter 2, Staffers have low defensive capabilities but are able to use a whole range of offensive attacks, ranging from light weapons to heavy artillery. Staffers are not able to defend themselves very well, because, as we have learnt earlier in the Introduction, Staffers are Staffers because they are not trusted to have the interests of the organization in mind. The organization keeps them at that level because the organization is aware that they are primarily interested in maximizing remuneration and job satisfaction while minimizing effort. In terms of offensives, Staffers have a whole arsenal at their disposal. We have discussed how Gossipmongers use gossip to get their way in the office. That's one type of light offensive. Gossips can always be denied by the Gossipmonger. Imagine throwing a stone at someone's window and walking off with our hands in our pocket. When confronted, we can always deny ever throwing that stone. "Could have been anyone along the street," we say, "why, could even have been that fella who over there… go ask him". Various other light offensives can be used, such as deliberately excluding a hated colleague from lunch invitations and delaying email responses to hated colleagues. Staffers can also use heavy artillery. Whistle blowing. That's one major offensive right there. Publicly declaring to colleagues and Management that they will not work with a certain colleague. That's another major offensive right there. Many others exist.

So when a colleague declares war publicly on us, what can we do? Always remember that even if the social contract is broken, there is still that legal contract in the workplace. As such, we can put this legal contract to good use. I have heard of some people who are so devastated by one colleague's actions that they end up leaving the organization. We don't have to do anything so drastic. Really, we don't. If we do, guess who will win? Yup, that very colleague who had put us in that very position.

So, how can we put this legal contract to good use? One way to do this is to take recourse to formalese for every work context. Use business language even in conversation. When confronted with fighting words, we cannot go wrong with phrases such as "Noted, with thanks" or "Thank you for your feedback". In that manner, we are putting up defenses without resorting to offense. Of course, one side effect of this is that it may infuriate our opponent more. Imagine the following conversation:

Opponent: "You did this to me!"

You: "Thank you for your feedback. Could you please explain further?"

Opponent: "I sent you an email... and you replied me late!"

You: "I note your concerns. May I know how I can help you further? Please advise."

Opponent: "Aaargh! Youuu!"

Now, that may not necessarily be a bad thing though. A hot head just gets hotter until it is beyond boiling point. Which brings me to my next point.

Another (more advanced) way to use the legal contract to our advantage is to bait our opponent into saying the wrong things. (Or the right things, depending on how we see it, to help our cause). So, do we get witnesses and lie in wait for the opponent to make a mistake?

No. Remember that we can't trust every colleague 100% of the time. Every colleague has the potential to Janus-ify, remember? Witnesses may not want to come forth for fear of reprisal. Witnesses may even turn around and play for the other team. Who knows what might influence them one way or another?

The best platform to get this done is the written platform, which includes email. Now, someone once told me, the best way to expose another person's flaws in reasoning is to ask him questions. Use this as bait. Take recourse to email communication. Pretend that you're really concerned and want to know more about how you can help him. Keep pretending not to understand, until he explains everything thoroughly, including the facts of the case, as he understands it, and how he feels about it. Then, say "let me see if I understand you correctly", and tell a completely different story. Sit back and watch the expletives fly. Save all of that and keep it as ammo. That will serve you very well, if you're willing to give it a shot.

But why would a colleague declare war? Shouldn't colleagues all try to get along? After all, we're all just here to make a decent living aren't we? Well, there are several reasons why a colleague would declare war. The first reason is that they're acting according to emotion. Simple enough. They hate your guts. They tell it to your face. Next thing you know, the whole office knows. Half of them are already placing bets on who delivers the knockout punch. The second reason, as a direct opposite of acting emotionally, is that they're acting rationally. Declaring war is a rational act indeed. When colleagues are fighting for the same set of resources, sometimes there are just not enough resources to satisfy all of them. To secure these resources, colleagues would thus declare war on each other. Imagine this very common situation. Three colleagues are up for promotion. There's one spot up there, a much coveted spot that all three are eyeing. Do you honestly think that they are going to shake each other's hands, wish each other luck and give their best individual effort? No, not everyone is as honest as that. More likely than not, each of them will be doing a "see-saw", that is, to pump up their good qualities while pushing down the other two. They might even declare war by deliberately trying to point out the others' incompetence, exposing their inadequacies or bringing to light their past indiscretions. All for the sake of that one coveted promotion that they each desire. Another rational reason for declaring war is for the purposes of signaling. In biology, signaling refers to behavior or characteristics that give information to potential mates, potential prey and potential predators. The peacock struts and displays its plumage to tell potential peahens that it is available to mate. The granular poison frog signals to potential predators with its bright red color that its flesh probably tastes quite awful, and thus, it shouldn't be eaten. In the workplace, a certain colleague might declare war on another to signal to others that he is not to be trifled with. He would thus choose his enemy well, an enemy whose defeat will be visible enough to be noticed. By noticing the defeat of that colleague, other potential predators lurking in the shadows would be scared off, giving the colleague who had declared war some measure of peace, at least for a while.

So, when should we declare war? Be careful about declaring war, I must warn you. As the saying goes, if you spit, you better mean it. This is because war does take a toll on us, on our opponents and on the other colleagues who might be caught in the crossfire. War has a high cost of transaction. According to Oliver E. Williamson, who was mentioned earlier, every transaction has an imputed cost. These might include the cost of searching for information, the cost of exchanging information and the cost of managing knowledge, among many others. When we declare war, we are paying costs for many, many transactions. These include transactions such as collecting information about the opponent, making alliances with other colleagues, reporting such information to Management and preparing for confrontations with the opponent. All these are qualitative indeed. There is no direct price to be set on, say, going through email threads to search for that one incriminating statement.

So, what's wrong with transaction costs? Well, they cost us time, effort and cognitive load. We need to spend time to conduct all these transactions. They don't just fall into our lap. We also need to spend effort collecting this information, effort which could have been spent doing other things. We also need to think about the transactions we're about to make, and to understand how to use the gains from these transactions to our advantage. Not to mention that war is high risk, so if we don't win that battle, all these costs would have gone to waste!

But here's a quick way to estimate these various qualitative costs such as "transaction costs", "search and information costs" and "sunk costs". First, take your salary per year. Divide that by 365 days. That's how much your life is worth for every day that you live. Break it down to the hour. Go ahead. Divide that by 24. That's how much money you potentially lose with every hour that you waste. So if your value is $x$, hey, that's $x$ lost every time you take that hour-long commuter train and just stare into space. That's also the cost of spending one hour making alliances, monitoring one's opponent, searching through email threads, and the like. That's assuming there is negligible cognitive load and emotional strain involved. If you find that making alliances, monitoring your opponent and such takes a toll on you, and you need to rest for an hour after every hour spent doing just those, that's another $x$ imputed, making it $2x$. Multiply that by the amount of time you think you need to prepare for war, fight the war and recover from war. It might just cost you an arm and a leg.

So, before we declare war, think about three main things. These three things are very important to our warring cognition. Chip and Dan Heath, in their book *Switch*, also offered three aspects of cognitive decision making, represented by "The Rider", "The Elephant" and "The Path". Here, I offer three similar aspects of cognitive decision making, namely, "The Attacker", "The Opponent" and "The Battlefield".

Firstly, "The Attacker" refers to any of us, just at the point of pondering whether to declare war or not. As the Attacker, we need to calculate the amount of resources we have to engage in war for that period of time that we think the war is going to last.

These resources will serve as our offense and defense. These resources include, as mentioned above, documentation, witnesses, opportunities for seeking redress and our own resolve to see things through. General Robert E. Lee's surrender to General Ulysses S. Grant during the American Civil War arguably was due to the depletion of the resources of his Confederate Army. Just as importantly, many a time, armies surrender because their Commanders do not have the resolve to wait the battle out. According to Stephen Sears, one of the controversies surrounding Major-General George B. McLellan of the Union Army during the American Civil War was that he was hesitant to commit to battle because he was too concerned with the morale and well-being of his soldiers.

Secondly, "The Opponent" is the person who we are considering declaring war upon. We need to make an educated guess on the state of resources of the opponent. Does he have more resources than we do? Better resources? Remember, never ever bring a knife to a gunfight. A knife is a short-range weapon. A gun can do damage at short-range, medium-range and long-range. Much more damage than a knife can do at short-range, I can tell you that. Do not engage an opponent who has more and better resources than we do. If we are not assured of victory, then all the costs we paid in the transaction leading up to and during the war would have gone to waste.

Thirdly, "The Battlefield" are the channels through which we are seeking to wage war. We need to ensure that we are familiar with the terrain to make battle. Jungle warfare is far different from urban warfare is far different from tundra warfare, as we can imagine. In the workplace, there are many channels in which we can fight battles. We can fight battles just between colleagues of the same level alone, or we can get Management involved (will be revisited in Chapter 2 under "Management as Mediator"). We need to understand that fighting a battle between colleagues of the same level is a different terrain than fighting a battle with Management involved. Even just between colleagues, fighting a battle with impressionable colleagues is different from fighting a battle with colleagues who already are allied one way or another. When we involve Management, it gets even more complicated. We need to be sure that Management is willing to give us a fair hearing rather than being dead set against our cause. Don't ever expect Management to be magnanimous and fair. Managers possess their own social, emotional and cognitive biases, which can very well spell trouble for us.

One major influence on the terrain of the battlefield is the organizational culture. Some organizations are discursively "harsher" than others at first glance. One example of this is the organization that the Wolf of Wall Street was working for, where curse words fly freely, and talk of autoeroticism occur openly among colleagues over lunch. Some organizations are discursively more "civil" than others at first glance. A religious organization, for example, where modesty and morals are to be observed at all times, demonstrates restraint in words chosen and actions taken. What am I getting at here? Don't bring thick clothing to war in the tropics, and don't bring a machete to a war in the tundra. As one would imagine, fighting a war in a religious organization using words and actions familiar to a "harsher" type organization would fail miserably.

It is not impossible to fight in the workplace as a lonesome Jonah Hex. In fact, lonesome fighters-against-the-world are quite legendary in Wild Western folk tales and post-apocalyptic literature. But sometimes, as the Beatles said, we get by with a little help from our friends, and the next section tells us how we can get it.

## MAKING ALLIANCES

Some of us like to work alone. Some of us like to work with others. Some of us are forced to work with others because our companies are so convinced that teamwork is the key to productivity. In any which case, when it comes to war, we sometimes must make alliances. Sometimes. At other times, we have to be like Rambo. All alone against the cruel world.

Why do we need to make alliances sometimes? Simply put, we need to leverage on the resources or the position of other colleagues who we might consider as potential allies. We need to make alliances with colleagues who are aware of office gossip, colleagues who are handling certain key projects, and sometimes even colleagues who are close to Management. Oftentimes though, we find that the colleagues who we find we most easily ally with are colleagues who share a common enemy. That's right. Nothing unites as much as a common enemy. Common enemies are often the topic of discussion when colleagues have tea or lunch together. Each will share what they do not like about this enemy, and they would in turn like to do to this enemy. They will all then shake their heads and say consoling things such as "That's not fair", or "He'll get his just desserts someday".

Making alliances is easy. It can be done either through a formal treaty of sorts, through an olive branch extended in the name of work, or through a social extension of the working relationship. One could, for example, clearly state to a potential ally that one would like to make an alliance. The advantage of this is that the alliance can be clarified at the onset. The disadvantage of this is that the potential ally might be turned off by one's brazenness in even offering that alliance. Alliances are a subtle game, you see, much like dating. One can't simply go up to any person at the bar and say, "Hey. I think you look good. I want to pick you up.

Do you agree?" That would be most likely met with a "Ewww, go away!" In order to pick a person up (either at a bar, at a library or at an Alcoholics Anonymous meeting), one has to feign disinterest while thinking of something common to build that bridge with and then ever so subtly introduce the idea of a possible exploration into the romantic side. Beware, though. "Lunch, sometime?" is not a romantic solicitation. At least not on Planet Earth.

A less direct way would be to extend an olive branch in the course of work. Offer to help that potentially ally, or say something like "I agree with the point raised by so-and-so" during meetings. In doing so, one is making a subtle hint that there is a bridge being built. Further help and further public agreements would add construction to that bridge.

Another less direct way would be to extend that working relationship to lunch or even after-work drinks. This way, one could build an alliance by demonstrating reciprocity, or in a lay phrase, "I scratch your back, you scratch mine". Reciprocity can be demonstrated during an alliance either by helping each other in the practical aspects of work, or by sharing similar emotions and understanding.

Bear in mind though, that not every colleague we wish to ally with would in turn agree to ally with us. One would make or break an alliance for several reasons. Firstly, that potential ally doesn't quite agree with us. He feels that by allying, he'd stand to lose more than gain. He is thinking rationally. No one wants more loss than gain. If he thinks that we are not to be trusted, he will see that allying with us might blow up in his face and bring potential loss. If he thinks that being seen with us would make the other colleagues think lesser of him, that would also mean potential loss. Secondly, that potential ally is already allied with Management or our opponent. By allying with us, he'd gain nothing, because all the resources that he needs at the workplace has already been provided by his current ally. The only way we'd be able to break his alliance and forge one with us is to offer him more and better resources than the other fella has. Thirdly, that potential ally is afraid of an alliance. He defines his ecological niche as one that is zen, peaceful and away from the maddening crowd. He can't see the benefit of the alliance, and he sees huge repercussions should the alliance not work in his favor. This kind of colleague is known as "The Non-Competitive One", who will be discussed in the next section.

## THE NON-COMPETITIVE ONES

At this point, some of us would be saying, "But I don't compete. Seriously, I don't care for competition at the workplace. I just want to do my work and go home". Or, we might know a colleague who just doesn't care enough to play office politics, and just minds their own business. So how do we explain this phenomenon of non-competitive colleagues? Are they above the ecology of the workplace? Do they not think rationally and want to get maximum returns and satisfaction with minimal effort just like the rest of us? Do good things really happen to good people *insert dumb face*?

The answer to that is that they are not above the ecology of the workplace, and they do think rationally. But why do they not compete? They do not compete simply because their existential selves need different resources from the rest of our colleagues who are in constant competition with one another. While the rest of us are competing in the open niche, the Non-Competitive Ones are occupying a separate niche, one that is shielded from the intense competition. They have either carved out that niche by themselves existentially, or have been placed in that comfortable niche by their patrons. By which I mean, they have either convinced themselves that they do not need to engage in competition in order to be happy at the workplace, or their patrons have put them in a place of protection such that they don't even need to go at it with the rest; their resources will be given to them as scraps from the Master's table.

As an example, consider this scenario. Imagine all of our colleagues (including us) are clamoring to get this major project because it means that the one who wins the project gets his name on the map. The whole industry would hear of that person's name. The Non-Competitive Ones might not be interested in it because, hey, they are just not interested in getting their name on the map. They might be interested in another project that, perhaps, allows them to diversify their interests. That could mean more to them. Or it could be that they're already happy with the money they're making, and getting their name on the map means little to them. Or it could be that they find much more joy and satisfaction in their leisure endeavors on the weekends, so whatever they do at work is immaterial; they could be asked to clean out poop for the same pay, and they wouldn't give a poop. That's our rational brain at work right there. The Non-Competitive Ones have rationalized and have thus convinced themselves that they are not interested in the same set of resources the rest of the colleagues are. But sometimes, something happens to shake that niche and affect the resources therein. Should that happen, the Non-Competitive Ones will use their rational brains yet again and do one of two things. They would either move out of that niche and go into another niche, or they would fight tooth and nail to maintain control of that niche. For example, say they're happy at work because it allows them to go home at their desired time. All of a sudden, one of their colleagues leaves, and the Non-Competitive One has to do her share of the work. That forces them to stay behind at work beyond the time they usually leave for home. That niche of theirs has just been invaded. What can they do? They can either protest taking on her work (fighting to maintain the niche) or will take on her work but ask for more pay (shifting their resources base from "time to leave work" to "remuneration"). In the first instance, this Non-Competitive One has just engaged his "fight" response, and competed to maintain control of that niche. In the second instance, this Non-Competitive One has engaged his "flight" response, and adapted to another niche. While the former requires external, outward resistance, the latter requires a fair bit of internal coping mechanisms, so that the existential self is convinced that adapting to that new niche will not bring about disbenefit.

For the Non-Competitive Ones who have been placed in their little niches by their patrons, though, how lucky of them. Their resources have been bestowed onto them, without the need for intense competition. In ecology, this patronage is referred to as the "host-parasite" relationship. The parasite latches on to the host, who in turn provides resources for the parasite. In many instances, the parasite does favors in return for the host, making the relationship "symbiotic", that is, mutually beneficial. One thing that I must caution, if we are in this sort of niche, though, is that we cannot take the security of this niche for granted. A niche provided by a patron is often turbulent for a few reasons. Firstly, the patron has power over us. His raised hand can bless us, or condemn us. Oftentimes, patrons require constant tributes. Tributes bring about blessings. If at any time, our actions are construed as a threat to the patron's existence, our heads are quite liable to roll. Secondly, others might try to take our place in this niche as the one the patron favors. They will compete with us because they see much benefit in being under that patron's patronage. We might thus end up being displaced and left high and dry. Thirdly, patrons are often called on to take on new responsibilities. When they leave, they take the niche with them. They may not take us with them, though, and without that niche, we would have to start learning to fend for ourselves. Fourthly, big names have big enemies. Our patron is likely to have as many supporters as he does enemies. And when these enemies try to get to him, there is a likelihood that they will attack us first. Why? As the legend of Keyzer Soze in *The Usual Suspects* illustrates, the best way to punish a person is by hurting his wife and children. Hurting someone's wife and children will hurt the person infinitely more than hurting the person directly. The enemies of our patrons will see us as our patron's "child". If any of this happens, we must be prepared to move on to another niche, even if it means having to compete for the resources just like everyone else.

No, good things don't happen to good people. The toast that falls out of our hands doesn't land butter side up. We all do what we have to do to observe the Darwinian law of the workplace jungle.

# CHECKPOINT ONE

We've reached the end of the first chapter. What have we discussed so far? We know that there are several archetypes of colleagues, with different characteristics stemming from how they rationalize their maximization of individual remuneration and satisfaction, and minimization of effort. We've categorized colleagues into the archetypes of "The Gossipmonger", "The Whisperer", "The Keyboard Warrior", "The Mouse", and a rather diverse category of "The Captains of Incompetence". These archetypes are neither exhaustive nor mutually exclusive. One could be a combination of two or more of these archetypes. And there are also other archetypes of colleagues which have not been included here. Where would we place a colleague who is genuinely nice and non-assuming, for example? In none of these archetypes, I would imagine. But such a type of colleague is not someone who is going to play an awfully important role in the workplace war anyway, and so his type has been omitted from the pages above. Don't forget the Januses, though. They're faceless and nameless, and can appear without warning. Let the cover of this book remind us that every colleague carries a briefcase in one hand, and a knife in the other. That knife can very well land in our backs.

We've also looked at what happens during a declaration of war, and how to survive when someone declares war on us. I've preached caution in declaring war ourselves because I certainly do believe that in most instances, we must always fight a battle that we know we can win. This is because wars cost resources (well, real wars cost lives too, but we're not killing anyone here are we?) and that takes a toll on us, as well as our opponent and our allies. We can always put up defenses, though, or conduct espionage to collect information on our opponent, or plan little sabotages, but an outright declaration of war is not very advisable unless we are certain we can win. In the next chapter, we'll cover more on the offensive tools we can use, as well as our defenses (this goes under the section "Fighting Capabilities"). Don't forget that offense and defense are two sides of the same coin. At times, a good offense may be our best defense. In other words, we strike before we are struck. At other times, a good defense may be parried into an offense. At yet other times, having the best defense would mean that we can withstand any siege by any invading army.

We've also covered the curious case of colleagues who do not compete. They do not compete because they are just not interested in the same resources that the rest are competing for. For a variety of reasons, these colleagues are satisfied with other resources that they're getting, and are hence non-competitive, at least with the others. They choose to not compete with the others because they have rationally evaluated their position, and deemed that there is no need to compete. Yet, when there is a threat to these resources they covet, their rational mind will again spring into action to retain said resources, or to evolve to tap on a new set of resources.

# CHAPTER 2: HOW TO SURVIVE HORRIBLE BOSSES

In *Horrible Bosses* and *Horrible Bosses 2*, Nick (played by Jason Bateman), Dale (played by Charlie Day) and Kurt (played by Jason Sudeikis) decide to take the law into their own hands and teach their horrible bosses a lesson. Taking advice from Motherfucker Jones (played by Jamie Foxx), the actions of the quartet can only be described as "stupid is as stupid does", following the famous line from *Forrest Gump*.

Now, our own Bosses in the workplace may not be as horrible as these, and we certainly should not commit murder or kidnapping, but the workplace war zone, with its ecological competition and rationally-minded employees has led some Bosses (or I guess, more appropriately, Managers) to become pretty horrible in their own right. Managers share one single imperative, as will be demonstrated below, but their own rational calculations and self-preserving nature lead them to adopt different archetypes and behave in different ways.

## THE MANAGERIAL IMPERATIVE

All Managers are the same.

Well, not exactly the same in every regard, obviously. Managers differ in behavior, emotion and cognition, but all Managers share the same imperative. They are all concerned with maximizing productivity from and minimizing remuneration to Staffers. Cynical, you say? Consider this example. Would a Manager want a Staffer to sell $100 worth of items and pay that Staffer $200 for that work done? No. Would a Manager want a Staffer to sell $200 worth of items and pay that Staffer $100 for that work done? Hell, yeah. Even better if the Staffer would accept $99. "Say, how about $80? Oh, you'll settle for $80? Let's make it $75 with possible performance bonus."

What about the Managers who always promote the idea of the workplace being a family? They give off a warm vibe don't they? They want everyone in the workplace to feel at ease don't they? The quick answer to that is that yes, they do sell the idea of the workplace-as-family, but yet the imperative remains. They want to purposefully give off a warm vibe and make everyone in the workplace at ease because they want to maximize productivity from and minimize remuneration to Staffers. They just feel differently about the workplace and behave differently towards Staffers, as compared to that Manager above whose only concern is money. This will be delved into in Chapter 3 under "One Big Happy Family", but for now, let me summarize quickly how being a family maximizes productivity from and minimizes remuneration to Staffers. By being a family, Staffers would feel obliged to do their best. Management does not have to worry about spending effort to motivate them. By being a family, Staffers would offer help unconditionally. Management does not have to worry about spending effort building up team cohesion. By being a family, Staffers would pick up each other's slack willingly. Management does not have to worry about keeping track of individual effort. By being a family, Staffers would not ask for more than necessary. Management does not have to spend money on extra incentives. By being a family, Staffers would not be cold and calculative. Management would get extra work done at no additional cost. By being a family, Staffers would forgive each other's indiscretions. Management would not have to mediate between contending Staffers. By being a family, Staffers would be open with each other. There would be no secrets. There would be no surprises. As far as Management hopes, there would be no chance of a mutiny!

Fact of the matter is, this whole workplace-as-family spiel is just another version of the Managerial Imperative to maximize productivity from and minimize remuneration to Staffers. Barring family businesses, I would argue that workplaces do not function in a true family-like manner. If they did, I'd be allowed to walk around the office-house-whatever in my underwear wouldn't I? I'd be allowed to fart at the lunch table wouldn't I? I'd be allowed to laze around and not do any work, wouldn't I? (Note to critics: Yes, I am aware I am setting up a strawman argument here. It was *takes a deep breath* deliberate). Oh, by the way, if you're interested in reading up more on family businesses, there is a ton of literature on family business models before the Industrial Revolution, large family corporations and family businesses in Asia.

"And what about the Managers who are sincere about developing us, huh?" I hear you say. "They're willing to invest in our skills upgrading and personal development. Why, I just purchased a ticket to the Maldives and my company paid for me!" Again, I will tell you that it is all in the name of productivity. While it is quite easy to keep us employees on the factory belt churning out product after product, some Managers are quite cognizant that fatigue will set in, and productivity will drop. They are also cognizant, from a more strategic point of view, that the company will reach a plateau if it keeps producing the same product year after year. Companies must evolve into producing value-added goods to move into bigger and more lucrative markets. Fatigue decreases productivity. Plateaus limit revenue. So, in order to increase productivity and revenue, companies have decided that investing a little bit in professional and personal development would increase productivity and revenue multiple-fold. See? It's not you they're concerned about. They're always concerned about their own imperative of maximizing productivity from and minimizing remuneration to Staffers. Here's another example. This one is from history, just to drive home this point.

All the way back in 1930, classical economist John Maynard Keynes predicted that by 2030, the average workweek would have reduced to about 15 hours. Technology would have developed so much, according to Keynes, that machines would have taken over most of the work tasks we humans had to do manually in 1930. The development of automation would thus become a boon to us, allowing us more freedom from work. Imagine having to work only 15 hours a week!

2030 is not too far away. Yet, we're not even coming close to working 15 hours a week. The lucky ones among us work 40 hours a week. Others, way more. So, what happened to the 15-hour workweek? Why has it eluded us? The answer lies in the Managerial Imperative. Management is intent on maximizing productivity. Always. True, much of our work processes have been automated, for example, in the textile industry. But new jobs which require human input continually get created in other industries. These new jobs require continual productivity, and the Managerial Imperative sees to it that productivity is always maximized. There is always more to be done. Thus, we're still working as many hours as we used to way back when Keynes made this prediction. Some of us, way more.

## TYPES OF MANAGERS

Let's get into our classification of Managers right now, just as how we did for colleagues above. Now, granted that there will be some overlap between the colleague archetypes and the Management archetypes, but what I am trying to show here are the archetypes that people assume in their role as Managers per se, and not as colleagues.

In this chapter, we'll take a look at the fearsome Machiavellian Manager, who rules with an iron fist, The Bross, a Boss who treats his Staffers like a bro, The Simulator, whose manages from a distance, most usually through memos and emails, and The Artful Dodger, whose cunning bars none.

These archetypes can indeed be compounded with the archetypes of colleagues that we discussed in Chapter 1. A Keyboard Warrior can assume the role of a Simulator in his management capacity. An Actor can assume the role of an Artful Dodger in his management capacity. A continua of various permutations is indeed possible.

# THE MACHIAVELLIAN MANAGER

"It is better to be feared than loved", said Niccolo Machiavelli in *The Prince*. Machiavelli believes that love is fleeting while fear is lasting. The effects of love are uncertain, while fear commands loyalty.

The Machiavellian Manager certainly believes in that. And they certainly embody that in their actions. The Machiavellian Manager makes a practice of instilling fear in the hearts and minds of Staffers.

Their terrifying presence is omniscient. Staffers cower at the very sight of them. Any email they send out must be answered within five minutes. And if they summon you while you're having lunch, drop your damn fork and hustle to their office. They want to see you that instant, and there are no two ways about it.

By creating a culture of fear, Machiavellian Managers are setting up the workplace as a niche where they are at the top of the food chain. They are the Alpha and Omega. The end all and be all. It's their show and we're mere actors on their stage. They have convinced their existential selves that there will be costs incurred by being less fearful, and that fear ensures productivity.

But, as the old adage goes, when the cat is away, the mice will come out to play. Fear can only be sustained by constant monitoring and the threat of major repercussions. Constant monitoring without the threat of repercussions does not work, and neither does the threat of repercussions without constant monitoring.

In *The Birth of the Prison*, Michel Foucault highlights us to the idea of a circular prison where prisoners are under constant supervision by guards and threatened with disciplinary punishment should they be seen breaking the rules. This is where there was constant monitoring and the threat of major repercussions. Imagine, however, if the guards were to sit and idly watch as the prisoners picked their locks and filed down their bars. Or if the guards were to proclaim that any escape attempts would be met by pain of death, but no monitoring of the prisoners was done. This culture of fear would then not meet its intended objectives. In the workplace, Machiavellian Managers would have to keep a watchful eye at all times, along with constant reminders of the punishments that await those who cross the line that they have drawn in the sand. One way Machiavellian Managers do this is to be always present and visible at the workplace. Another way is to recruit Whisperers to clue them in to the happenings on the ground so that they can be aware and jump on any issues that crop up. More on maintaining a culture of fear and coercive restraint can be read in Ian Baptiste's work "Beyond Reason and Personal Integrity".

Machiavellian Managers do not send others to do their dirty work for them. No, they enjoy being the bearers of bad news too much. It gives them such great pleasure to play the role of the disciplinarian and put Staffers in their place. They're neutral to good news though. They can deliver good news, but they don't necessarily have to. They don't care about being the good guy, you see.

Machiavellian Managers want us to recognize their superiority. They will not tolerate any deviation from this intended relationship. Their ultimate objective is to have us refer to them in honorific terms, openly show our respect and follow their orders. Try to treat them like peers, and they will put us in our place. Try to treat them like family and they will put us in our place. Their image resembles a monolith that cannot be changed. Not without resorting to certain pressures, of course, as will be shown below under the "Caveat Lector".

Now, why would a Manager adopt a Machiavellian persona? Firstly, they could be cognitively aligned to such an archetype. Simply put, they can see no other way of being a Manager. They are likely to be convinced that being Machiavellian is the only way to Manage. It would take a lot of cognitive reformatting to convince the Machiavellian Manager who is cognitively convinced that there are other management styles. Sometimes, the Machiavellian Manager does eventually realize that this style doesn't work in all instances. But that would take quite a bit of pressure, sometimes from within, and sometimes from without. Again, we'll look at this in more detail under "Caveat Lector".

Secondly, they could also perhaps see that Staffers need them more than they need Staffers. Such situations occur when, for example, the Manager has demonstrated competency beyond everybody else, and has been recognized to possess such "expert" level status. It could also be that the organization in question is in an industry which has high barriers to entry coupled with an oversupply of job applicants. The Machiavellian Manager of this sort is more fluid than the sort who cognitively is locked into the Machiavellian mode. He is able to manage in ways other than Machiavellian, but he simply chooses to do so because he can.

Disclaimer. The term "Machiavellian Managers" is not a new term I coined, sorry to disappoint you. Many others have used this term as well. For example, a similar term, "Machiavel", was used by Oliver James in his book *Office Politics*. This term is pretty much fair game, just like a Commons, if you recall from our discussion earlier.

## THE BROSS

The Bross refers to a Boss (or Manager) who treats Staffers like a bro. He may literally call his Staffers "bro". He may also act like a cool Manager and tries to have casual conversations with his Staffers. Another thing he might do is to insist that Staffers call him by his first name. And oftentimes, he'd impose himself on Staffers for lunch and such. Sounds familiar? The Bross is a relatively recent phenomenon. Bosses never used to be Brosses until quite recently.

Behaviorally, the Bross is the exact opposite of the Machiavellian Manager. Instead of a culture of fear, the Bross wants to promote a culture of cordiality by acting like a friend rather than a disciplinarian. While the Bross does not see the need to occupy a superior position in the niche to have advantage, the Managerial Imperative remains. Brosses have rationally calculated that by being a bro, they'd be stimulating productivity. They don't really want to be our bro for real. They want to be our bro because they think that by pretending to be our bro, we'll do better at work. Try becoming less productive by, for example, skiving or sleeping on the job. The Bross won't be yo bro no mo.

Brosses love to be the bearer of good news only. They can't bring themselves to bring bad news, so they're more likely than not get someone to do their dirty work for them. Any disciplinary issues, or anything to do with a reduction in salary or benefits will not come from Brosses. They'd get someone else to relay such news to us. Oh, and Brosses love promises. They are quick to tell us how well we're doing, and how much they appreciate our help at work, and how we are definitely in a for a bro-nus or a bro-motion.

But why would a Manager choose to adopt a Bross persona, as compared to say, a Machiavellian Manager persona? A Bross persona is usually adopted for one of two reasons. Firstly, the organization has a philosophy that a more casual management style would stimulate productivity. An exemplar of this philosophy is, of course, Google Inc. This organization is famous for having sleeping pods to take power naps in, free meals for employees and bicycles to travel around the Googleplex on (refer to article on "Google's Corporate Culture" in *The Economist*). Another notable organization is 3M, whose innovation is said to stem from the "15% time" rule, where employees get to work on non-official work tasks for 15% of the time they spend at work in a week (see Arndt's article on 3M in *Bloomberg*).

Secondly, the Bross himself thinks that a more casual management style would help him maximize productivity from his Staffers. He is probably aware that he needs to appear friendly in order to tap into the knowledge and skills of the Staffers. He might not possess enough knowledge and skills to have an edge over the Staffers, and instead highly depends on them to complete the deliverables.

The Bross wants us to reci-bro-cate the bromance, bro. He would feel oh so very dejected if we were to treat him in any way other than a bro. Much like a jilted suitor, Brosses would feel down if we were to extend invitations to our other colleagues and exclude him. Brosses would feel sad if we were to show any indication of being uncomfortable around them. Just for fun, try to refer to them by rank (such as "Assistant Director") or an honorific (such as "Sir") instead of by name and watch their faces crumble. Tell them you're "not comfortable fraternizing with management" and listen for that tiny crack in their heart. When they're within earshot, make arrangements with your close colleagues for a "Staffer-only lunch". Stand at attention whenever they walk by, for added effect. A word of caution when trying these little office hacks though. Don't let them know. They see us trollin', they be hatin'.

## THE SIMULATOR

I've had a few choices in naming this archetype. I toyed with The Silent Killer, The Delegator, The Fortifier, but settled on The Simulator because of its Freudian proximity to the image of an adult ladies' toy. Essentially, the Simulator manages at a distance instead of up close. More often than not, Simulators use memos and email to do their bidding. They will send us information they'd like us to note, orders for action to be taken and chastisement for "inappropriate behavior". Yup, all over email. The most efficient way of communication. At least to The Simulator.

More often than not, these distant notes are not accompanied by explanations and rationale. They would certainly not be followed up with a telephone call or a face-to-face chat. Staffers who are Keyboard Warriors easily assume the persona of the Simulator if they get promoted to Management level (we discussed Keyboard Warriors in Chapter 1). But Simulators are not exclusively born of Keyboard Warrior pedigree. Simulators can also be made. A Manager can assume the archetype of a Simulator when it is rational for his existential self to do so.

How does that happen? The Simulator would have calculated the amount of effort taken to communicate with Staffers using various communication channels, such as face-to-face, telephone or email. He'd calculate the opportunity cost of each method of communication. He would think, for example, that a face-to-face meeting to explain one task would take him, perhaps a half hour. In that half hour, he could send ten emails to ten different Staffers with ten different tasks. Rationally, he would choose the email method. Look, it's ten times the amount of work done for the same amount of time! The Simulator would then get the impression that managing at a distance would cost him less effort than by more direct means. That would be enticing to him, rationally speaking.

Simulators can exist anywhere, really. We can find them in small companies and large companies, in situations of high employment and low employment, in male-dominated organizations and female-dominated organizations. Simulators, however, are encouraged by sheltered communication channels which they can take refuge in. An organization which has a memo-friendly or email-friendly culture tends to stimulate the growth of Simulators. This is because sheltered communication channels are one of the resources that Simulators need in order to function in organizations. They're kind of like the fungus that grows in sewers.

Simulators don't really care either way for good news or bad. They'll just relay that information from a distance anyway. What Simulators want most out of their relationship with Staffers is for that distance to be maintained. Unlike the pawn on a chessboard who gallantly tries to engage with the other pieces, Simulators are like the Queen piece in an endgame. Move close and the Queen will run to the other corner. Come close again and the Queen scoots off to the opposite corner. They hate confrontation, these Simulators. It either makes them feel out of place (as is the case with Keyboard Warriors), or they don't like it because it is not worth their effort.

Either way, this is where we can have some fun. Instead of accepting the tasks, information and chastisement sent from a distance, kindly request for Simulators to meet us face-to-face to explain. Pretend that we don't understand. Pretend that we're intellectually challenged, if we have to. Just get them to meet us face-to-face, and see their faces turn sour. This sourness would be caused either by the discomfort of human interaction, or by having their precious minutes tick away as they explain everything in great detail to little ol' us. Make sure they explain every little detail please. That effort and time taken is very costly to their cognitive well-being.

## THE ARTFUL DODGER

And then we have the Artful Dodger. The Artful Dodger is a Manager who uses sly tactics to get his way with Staffers. Just like the real Artful Dodger, who appears as a pickpocket in Charles Dickens's book *Oliver Twist*, Managers who adopt this Artful Dodger persona are skilled in the art of deception. Keep in mind that the Artful Dodger type of Manager shares the same Managerial Imperative as any other Manager. There are no limits to the tricks that Artful Dodgers can play, but the following are some that I have been made familiar with:

Firstly, being "economical with the truth", as Atticus Finch articulately phrases it in *To Kill a Mockingbird*. Artful Dodgers do not tell outright lies. They just tell Staffers partial truths. These partial truths may include information about career opportunities, promotions, or even salary packages. By being economical with the truth, Artful Dodgers avoid being accused of lying. No sirree bob. They just "forgot" to put in certain details. Or they were just "phrasing" it in a different way.

Secondly, keeping Key Performance Indicators qualitative. Instead of giving a fixed guideline to follow, they state Key Performance Indicators in such a way that it can have multiple interpretations. Why do they do this? So that they can always justify their own assessment of Staffers' performance. Artful Dodgers want to maximize Staffers' productivity, but don't want Staffers to stop working as soon as Key Performance Indicators are met. And so, the most brilliant of brilliant plans were hatched. "Keep the Key Performance Indicators qualitative", Artful Dodgers thought, "so that we can always tell the Staffers that they have not done enough." And so, qualitative Key Performance Indicators such as "Demonstrate willingness to perform beyond expectation" and "Work well in a team" were created. There is no way to accurately measure "demonstrate", "willingness", "expectation" and "well", which means that Artful Dodgers could always say "you have not demonstrated enough", "I did not notice a great deal of willingness", "you did not meet my expectations" and "you did not work well enough". This familiar trick is also known as a "moving target" or "shifting goalposts".

Thirdly, giving faux empowerment. Management gurus such as Kevin Snyder suggest that empowered Staffers work harder because they feel that they "own" the project or task. Of course this idea of empowerment is not new. It has roots in Karl Marx's works on socialism, where he argues that the ownership of one's own means of production is the natural, proper state of affairs. It allows us humans to be normal "species beings". Marx goes on to argue that working for someone else is unnatural and departs from this species being of ours. But we all know that working for someone else is the best that most of us can do, don't we? For a variety of reasons, starting our own business may not be the smartest decision. So, let's discuss the idea of empowerment as employees of an organization. Now, empowerment is good. It is directly related to job satisfaction, which, as we mentioned earlier, is a motivation factor for us to perform at work. Empowerment can be given to us by, for example, allowing us to run projects independently, not breathing down our necks and co-opting us as part of the decision-making process. But giving Staffers power would mean that Artful Dodgers have to relinquish some of the power from themselves, wouldn't it? After all, power is, ceteris paribus, a zero-sum game. Power, in Physics, is the product of current and voltage. With no change to current or voltage, power remains constant. Similarly, in organizational behavior, power is a function of several variables. With no change to these variables, power remains constant. Power can be redistributed but not increased. But Artful Dodgers don't want to relinquish power from themselves! So how could they possibly increase productivity while retaining power? Why, by giving faux power, of course! One of the common ways in which Artful Dodgers give faux power is by continually asking for suggestions and inputs from Staffers on strategic matters, but not accepting any of those suggestions and inputs in practice (this will be revisited later in Chapter 3 under "Giving Suggestions"). When questioned about whatever happened to the suggestions and inputs given earlier, Artful Dodgers would say that all suggestions and inputs were considered, but the suggestion that best fits the interests of the organization was ultimately chosen. More likely than not, this "suggestion" that "fits the interests" probably came from the Artful Dodgers themselves. Rinse and repeat.

Artful Dodgers want you to believe their bullshit. They have prepared a million and one deflective defenses for any question anyone might have regarding their managerial skills, their relationship with Staffers and the organization. Artful Dodgers are sharp enough to guess what resources could be used to their advantage, and skillfully maneuver those resources around the Staffers. Good news, bad news, even non-news can be skillfully manipulated as a potential resource by Artful Dodgers.

Artful Dodgers, just like Simulators, can be found in almost any organization. It takes a certain level of intelligence for a Manager to adopt an Artful Dodger persona. A Manager who is not cognizant of what his Staffers know or feel cannot be a good Artful Dodger. I mean, he can certainly try to trick us, but we'll see through his lies in a jiffy. A Manager who is a naive as Forrest Gump surely cannot be an Artful Dodger too. He wouldn't know what a lie is if it hit him in the head.

For Artful Dodgers, their offensive strategies and their defensive strategies are one and the same (offense and defense will be covered in greater detail below). Try calling their bluff, and we'll be met with another bluff. We have to call it until there is nothing left to call for Artful Dodgers to admit that they've been bluffing us all along. Artful Dodgers are like onions, somewhat. They layer their trickery pretty thick. And peeling all those layers can make us cry. Us.

If Machiavellian Managers hate Staffers who disrespect their authoritahhh, and Brosses feel hurt by Staffers who reject their cordial approach to management, who do you think Artful Dodgers detest?

Artful Dodgers despise Staffers who are smart enough to see through their lies. You see, the control that Artful Dodgers have over their own lies can be seen as control over a resource. When those lies cease to work, Artful Dodgers get real antsy in their pantsy. Staffers who can call their bluffs essentially are robbing them of the resources they need to survive as Artful Dodgers. Even worse are Staffers who not only call their bluffs, but also are able to pull wool over their eyes. That be like Brer Rabbit, my friends. The trickster who can trick other tricksters and still come out safe and sound in the briar patch. Be's real careful like, though. Being a Brer Rabbit will sho'ly put yo name on a bullet. 'Specially when hunting season comes 'round.

## CAVEAT LECTOR

I must preach another caveat, just as I did with the archetypes of colleagues earlier. Of course there are many, many more archetypes of Managers than the ones shown here. We all have non-flattering nicknames we give to our Bosses, don't we? But perhaps some of these nicknames are just too common. Or just not interesting enough to deserve a main archetypal category. Or maybe even not horrible enough. The title of this chapter is "How to Survive Horrible Bosses", remember? As with the archetypes of colleagues above, those that I deem to not be important enough to be considered an archetypal category, I have deliberately left out.

One important thing to note about Managers, though, is that they are shape shifters. They can easily change from archetype to another. These changes are not caused by the full moon, though. These changes often occur as a reaction to two main factors, firstly, their rational sense of maximizing productivity from and minimizing remuneration to Staffers (change from within), and secondly, their sense of self-preservation vis-a-vis their own superiors (change from without).

The Managerial Imperative demands that Managers maximize productivity from and minimize remuneration to Staffers. Maximization and minimization, though, is never complete. It is an ongoing process, and for most of the time, there is always more to be done to move in the direction of more productivity, and less remuneration. Why else do you think automation exists in factories? High productivity, low maintenance. Why else do you think child labor, sweatshops, indentured labor, modern-day slavery, and all other forms of poorly remunerated labor exist? You guessed it. To maximize productivity and minimize remuneration. Now, we can consider any shape-shifting that occurs as a result of this process to be internal to the Manager. It is a result of his own reflection of his own Managerial strategies, and his own evaluation of what works and what doesn't.

Imagine this situation. A Machiavellian Manager breathes down the neck of his Staffers. He makes sure they come to work on time. Any lateness will be given a stern talking to. He makes sure they are at their desks toiling away during working hours. Any semblance of laughter or small talk between Staffers will be given a stern talking to too. After a week, he discovers that the Staffers have brought in $200 each on average, and were paid, gasp, $200 each. So he cuts their pay down to $100, and at the end of the next week, discovers that they have brought in $100. The Staffers are obviously practicing what is called as "making out", that is, they just do enough work for the amount that they're paid for. For a more colorful account of making out, see Michael Burawoy's work. Of course, Staffers would make out. Staffers are rational beings, as we have discussed in the preceding pages of this book. The rational Machiavellian Manager would then reflect and do one of two things. He'd either step up his Machiavellian Manager game even more, or he would thus shape-shift and take on the form of another archetype. He might try to be an Artful Dodger, or he might even try to be a Bross, just for the sake of maximizing productivity and minimizing remuneration. This depends on how he cognitively perceives himself, his motivation to change, and his ability to change. If he cognitively is convinced that being a Machiavellian Manager is the only way to manage, or if he is not motivated to change, or he simply cannot pull off another archetype, he will likely step up his game to become even more Machiavellian than before, instead of shifting shape to another archetype. But the reverse is true too. Managers who are cognitively not locked in to a certain archetype, are internally motivated to shift shape, and know how to shift shape, will certainly try to shift shape into another archetype.

The other reason why Managers would shape shift is external. The impetus for change comes from pressure from his superiors. Practically speaking, anyone with power over said Managers could indeed pressure them to change. That could mean their wives, a client or even a Staffer who looks physically intimidating. But for the sake of keeping in focus, let's focus on those Manager's superiors. We'll be discussing the different areas of focus for Managers of different ranks.

Now, we all know that Managers are after all, employees of an organization, the same organization as the Staffers who they're supposed to manage. That means that they get paid, just like Staffers do, and they have their own superiors that they report to, just like Staffers do. Managers certainly don't own the means of production, despite some companies' attempts to pretend that they do via employee stock ownership and whatnot. The only difference between Managers and Staffers is that Managers are empowered to be voices of the organization, and have to ensure that Staffers act in accordance with the philosophy, policies, procedures and practices of said organization. This idea of philosophy, policies, procedures and practices I borrowed from Degani and Wiener's work on aviation management. Let me try to explain.

Now, as Managers climb the ranks, they get further and further away from the ground. Their foci get less micro and more macro. To use more commonplace terms, the Most-Junior Manager has, in his sights, the practices of the Staffers on the ground. He can see who does what, who says what, and who comes in late. He is placed in that position to monitor such things on the ground, because those things are well within his sight. Oftentimes, these "junior" Managers get stuck in between being a Staffer and being a Manager. We'll revisit their plight under the section of "Sandwiched Managers" further down this chapter. The One-Rank-Above-Most-Junior Manager, on the other hand, does not see the ground so clearly. The objects on the ground look smaller, because the Next-Rank-Above-Most-Junior Manager has better sight of the procedures of the organization. He can't see who's drawing more stationery than needed, or who's having more sick days than desired, but he can see how to manage company property, leave entitlements and such. The Two-Ranks-Above-Most-Junior Manager has an even worse sight of the ground. The objects on the ground look small and blurry to him. He, however, has a pretty good view of the policies of the organization. The Commandments, if you will. The "Thou shalt Nots" and the "It is thy Rights". He is tasked not with watching the ground, but with enforcing and justifying the Commandments of the organization. And the Most-Senior Manager? He has pretty much no sight of the ground. Objects on the ground look like ants to him. He doesn't have such a great sight of the procedures either. His focus is on the philosophy of the organization, that is, what the organization stands for. He justifies the raison d'etre of the organization. He maintains contact with other organizations of similar philosophies. And he maintains a separation with organizations with opposite philosophies. Commissioners of Police, for example, maintain contact with other Commissioners of Police. They could even come together through Interpol. Commissioners of Police maintain a clear separation (at least formally) between their own police corps and say, criminal organizations.

Now, philosophy informs policy, which in turn informs procedure, which in turn informs practice. As we can imagine, any change in philosophy will affect policy, any change in policy will affect procedure, and any change in procedure will affect practice. Any ripple of change anywhere high up in the ranks will affect how a Manager below deals with his Staffers. To maintain things the way they are would require a lot of effort on the part of said Manager to withstand the change. Most of the time, Managers will go along with the wave, and change accordingly. This change may take the form of a shape shift into another archetype.

Imagine this scenario. A Bross treats his Staffers like his bro. The Bross takes them out for lunch and even after-work drinks. They share stories like bros would. The Bross even allows his Staffers to work from home so that the time taken to commute could be put to more productive use. All of a sudden, the Bross's own superior tells him that the budget is being cut and that the Bross must ensure that each Staffer brings in increased profit revenue each week. No more long-term goals, no more people development policies to develop value-added products. The Bross's superior wants money now, now, now! What would the Bross do then? Well, he might try to withstand the winds of change by trying to convince his superior that long-term goals, people development and product development is still important. Hell, he might even soak up the extra work that needs to be done by himself just to shelter his Staffers from the blitzkrieg. How long can he keep this up? As long as he has resources and resolve, of course. This was discussed previously in Chapter 1 under "Declaration of War".

When he cannot keep this up no mo, the self-preserving Bross would change into one of the other archetypes in a desperate attempt to meet his superior's demands. "To hell with what the Staffers think. It's me or them", he'd rationalize with himself. The Bross could perhaps turn into a Simulator by cutting all engagements with his Staffers, and choosing instead to fire off orders in rapid succession through email. Time saved, a penny earned. Or he could turn into an Artful Dodger, by promising his Staffers a monetary bonus, extra manpower or any other rewards for helping to increase revenue. But as we all know, Artful Dodgers never really deliver their end of the bargain, but that's another story. The point here is that the shape shift to another archetype merely serves the self-preserving nature of the rational Manager.

## SANDWICHED MANAGERS

"Welcome to Subway. May I take your order?"

Haha, no, that's not what I mean by "Sandwiched Managers". Sandwiched Managers are the poor sods who have been given an official Managerial title, but are still treated as Staffers by the Managers above him. In practice, he is given the responsibilities of a Manager, but not the power. He is made to lead teams and ensure that work systems are always go. He is required to possess the Managerial Imperative, by continually trying to up the productivity of his Staff. Sometimes he's even made to sell the workplace-as-family spiel, just like any other Manager. Yet, he is not given the right to make significant decisions or influence change in the organization.

Why does this happen? Remember that discussion earlier we had on "trust"? We discussed how organizations co-opt employees into a hierarchy based on the level of trust they had for each employee. The least trusted fella goes right at the bottom. The most trusted fella goes right at the top. Sandwiched Managers are somewhere in between, but towards the bottom end. Sandwiched Managers are not completely trustworthy, according to the organization and higher Management. But Sandwiched Managers are trusted enough, just enough, to take responsibility over work tasks. More trustworthy than Staffers, at least.

A caricatured conversation between a Sandwiched Manager and his superior Manager might go a little bit something like this:

Superior Manager: "I need you to take ownership over this project. Take responsibility."

Sandwiched Manager: "Yes, Sir. Thank you for the opportunity. May I choose the Staffers I wish to work on this project with me?"

Superior Manager: "Err, no… I make that decision."

Sandwiched Manager: "But there's one Staffer in particular who's not quite right for this project. He just cannot keep up with the rest of his team mates. He's not quite skillful, and he's pretty slow at his tasks."

Superior Manager: "Well, manage him."

Sandwiched Manager: "How, Sir?"

Superior Manager: "Just manage him. You should take more responsibility over your Staffers!"

Sandwiched Manager: "May I suggest that he be redeployed elsewhere? He's not suited for this project."

Superior Manager: "Err… no, I make that decision."

The conversation above illustrates how the Sandwiched Manager gets the worst of both worlds. Staffers treat him like a Manager, but his own superior Manager treats him like a Staffer. That's the flip side to being a hybrid or a chimera, really. Some hybrids have the best of both worlds. We all know that a mule is a hybrid of a male donkey and a female horse. According to Jackson's book, the resultant hybrid has the best of both worlds. Mules exhibit the patience, speed and intelligence of horses and the sure-footedness, hardiness and longevity of donkeys. Nobody would want a hybrid that has the stubbornness, slowness and poor intelligence of donkeys coupled with the clumsiness, fragility and short life span of horses would they?

That would be the worst of both worlds indeed. Yet, the Sandwiched Manager is one such hybrid that has the worst of both worlds.

This inferior hybridization is reflected even in terms of fighting capabilities. Sandwiched Managers often have the defense capabilities of Staffers, but the offense capabilities of Managers. In other words, Sandwiched Managers have a poor defense system and can only use heavy artillery. Let me put an image to this. It's like having a soldier stand in the middle of the battlefield with no cover, and ordering him to fire cannons. The poor defense system of Sandwiched Managers means that they are not quite strong enough to defend themselves and those under their charge from attacks. This is why, as discussed above, they are unable to absorb the shocks from the superior Managers, and are thus forced to shape shift into a Managerial archetype that will help their superior Managers realize their vision for the organization.

In terms of offense, Sandwiched Managers can only rely on reproducible evidence and noticeable behaviors, just like the rest of Management can. Sandwiched Managers cannot engage in light attacks the way Staffers do. Staffers still think of Sandwiched Managers as "Management". And to superior Managers, Sandwiched Managers possess the formal title of "Manager". As such, it would not be awfully appropriate for Sandwiched Managers to engage in the same offensives as Staffers do. Sandwiched Managers cannot willy nilly give the cold shoulder to a colleague the way Staffers can. Sandwiched Managers cannot willy nilly engage in gossip or ostracization the way Staffers can. Sandwiched Managers are required to stand up for the interests of the organization and behave like any other Manager would.

The position of a Sandwiched Manager is not an enviable one. Their Managerial status is only visible in fair weather, and during fine-grained changes in the organization. When money is rolling in, everyone is motivated and every once in a while some inconsequential problem appears, hey, the Sandwiched Manager flies his flag proudly. He can stake his claim to being a member of the esteemed Management club in that organization. He is able to take ownership and responsibility over the projects he is made to oversee.

When the weather is kind of gloomy, and there are coarse-grained changes afoot, look out Sandwiched Manager, you gon get it. During times when the company is not making as much money, or when staff turnover is high, or when productivity is low, or when a new hotshot CEO has just stepped in to "spice things up a little", the Sandwiched Manager is not going to have a whale of a time. He'd be held accountable for the mistakes that were made. He'd be asked to justify why the projects under his charge are not performing as well as expected. He would be held responsible, no doubt. But the organization would exercise amnesia in conveniently forgetting that he was given neither significant decision-making power nor power to influence change in the first place. During these times, his Managerial position might even be overridden by his superior Manager, who decides to take the reins on the rocky road.

Say, just curious… how many of you identify yourselves as a Sandwiched Manager? People at work toggle between treating you as a Staffer and as a Manager, don't they? Not a good feeling, I agree.

## MANAGING MANAGEMENT

So far, we've made it pretty clear that Management and Staff can be seen as being diametrically opposed to each other. Management and Staff have very different interests from each other. Their rational minds work differently. And they occupy different niches in the workplace ecological system. Management is interested in maximizing productivity from and minimizing remuneration to Staffers. Staffers are interested in maximizing individual remuneration and satisfaction while minimizing effort. This suggests that Staff and Management are "natural enemies" because they're interested in taking away the very resources that each other needs. When natural enemies meet, it only takes a spark to start an inferno. Even between Staffers, conflict is imminent. As discussed in Chapter 1, the only Staffers who do not compete with the others are those who need a different set of resources, and those who are fed resources directly. All other Staffers come into conflict with each other in the mad rush to maximize remuneration and satisfaction while minimizing effort.

This section will discuss several characteristics of Management vis-a-vis Staff. It will discuss the concept of "group preservation" among Management and Staff, the fighting capabilities of Management and Staff respectively, alliances between Managers and Staffers and finally the actions of Management when they mediate between Staffers. It is hoped that by the discussion in this section, we will be better able to manage our Bosses.

## GROUP PRESERVATION

One phenomenon that keeps popping up time and again in my observation of organizations is the phenomenon of "group preservation" among Managers. "Group preservation" is a phenomenon in Darwinian ecology which states that organisms will seek to preserve their own species, because (very simplistically put), if their species were to ever go extinct, they would cease to exist too. I know, I know, this is a "truism", but as I said, this is the simplest way I can explain it. Kind of reminds me of that joke in the early 2000s: "Sex is hereditary. If your parents didn't have it, you wouldn't too."

For our context here, this means that "Management supports Management". Being vested with the powers of the organization, Managers tend to feel a certain bond with each other as compared to with the Staffers. I suppose from Schutz's "phenomenological psychology" point of view, there is an "inner experience" between Managers who can be considered "consociates" with one another. Consociates partake of each other's inner experience and live in a mutual relationship that entails a long-term shared experience. This is why it is very difficult for Staffers to complain about one Manager to another Manager. It won't work. In other words, go up against one Manager, and you go up against the entire Management. Managers, by and large, are united in their understanding that one of their key tasks is to command and control Staffers. This is also the reason why Whisperers exist. By allying closely with Management, they are hoping to be treated just like any other member of Management, and thus receive the same benefits of protection as other Managers do. Of course, between individual Managers, there will definitely be conflict. Masks are put on and backs are stabbed between different Managers, as it happens between different Staffers. However, divisions within the Management contingent will never be made known (at least explicitly) to Staffers. Management will always try to manage the impression Staffers have of the entire Management contingent.

What about the Staff contingent eh? One for all and all for one? Not at all. While the Management contingent practices group preservation, there is no similar phenomenon within the Staff contingent. Why is this? This is because Staffers do not share a mandate with each other. Staffers are primarily interested maximizing their own remuneration and satisfaction. In doing so, they're trying also to minimize their contribution to the pooled effort. No Staffer would be stupid enough to "take one for the entire team" by doing all the work so that the other Staffers can rest easy. No, way, Jose! The rational senses of each individual Staffer pushes each of them to keep their own individual equations balanced. More effort will be put in for tasks that will remunerate more and give more satisfaction. But a dip in the pay, and a loss of satisfaction will see a dip in effort made as well. Of course, Staffers don't count beans when it comes to the units of the equation. If they did, every single Staffer would be a Dazy Log (discussed above under "Captains of Incompetence"), wouldn't they? There is of course some level of give and take between Staffers, but this tends to happen within Staffer cliques only. This courtesy is not extended to the entire Staffer contingent. A Staffer who has allied with two others, for example, will cover their backs, because he knows that by covering their backs, he can expect them to reciprocally cover his in the future. But he won't be so kind as to cover every other Staffer's back as well. For one, what's in it for him to cover some other fella in some other team who he has met only once during Company Orientation? For another, if he were to cover this fella's back, can he trust this fella to not take advantage of his kindness? In other words, will this other fella cover his back in the future? He can't be sure of that. Will this other fella run and tell Management that he's been covering for others? He can't be sure of that.

But what does Management make of group preservation among Staff? Surely, Management would like Staff to also exhibit a sense of group preservation, innit? I mean, after all, since Management is trying very hard to sell the idea that the workplace is a family unit, shouldn't they encourage group preservation among Staff too? Logically, only with a sense of group preservation can the idea of the workplace-as-family be realized, right? Together we stand, divided we fall? Truth of the matter is, Management is quite wary of any kind of unity or alliance among Staffers. Management will only be supportive of the kind of unity that sings the same tune as they do, but will be uneasy of any other kind of unity among Staffers. A group of Staffers that continually sings praises to the organization's philosophy, policies, procedures or practices will be looked upon favorably by Management. A group of Staffers that continually reinforce the Managerial Imperative to each other will be looked upon favorably by Management. A group of Staffers that continually venerate the senior leaders of the organization will be looked upon favorably by Management. But a group of Staffers who band together just because they have common topics to talk about together will not be looked upon favorably. They will be seen as being exclusionary towards other Staffers who are not part of that group. A group of Staffers who continually discuss their disgruntledness towards other colleagues, Management, tasks or organizational theatrics will be frowned upon even more. Most of the time, these groups do not create the disgruntledness. These groups merely are a collection of already-disgruntled individuals who seek solace in each other. Without being a part of one of these groups, individuals would suffer in silence and would feel even more alienated towards the workplace. Their membership in these groups gives them a cathartic outlet by which they can share their disgruntledness, and diffuse their unhappiness away. They can also learn from each other on how to maneuver around certain dislikeable colleagues, dislikeable Managers or theatrical work. Yet, Management will still frown upon such groups because such groups do not appear to be happy and aligned with the Managerial Imperative.

So, what does the strong sense of group preservation among Management and the lack of group preservation among Staff mean for warfare? This means that it would be all too easy for Management to divide and conquer the Staffer contingent. It's like a national army going up against a group of mercenaries. Mercenaries are only interested in two things, namely, money and saving their own skin. They come from different places, have different experiences, and will seek to take care of only themselves. If the money is enough, they'll fight the battle. If it's too risky, they won't. And they sure as hell won't put their behinds in danger just to save another mercenary. Loyalty is not part of their creed. Money and self-preservation is. Soldiers from national armies, on the other hand, are co-opted into uniformity and made to swear loyalty to the country and to each other. They are made to wear uniforms to signify their membership, and wear insignia to represent their allegiance. They're organized into platoons for operational purposes, companies for tactical purposes and larger groupings (such as units or brigades) for strategic purposes. They are trained to watch each other's backs and maintain unity in order to win the battle.

Let's bring this back to the workplace context. Throughout history, and across the industrialized world, there have been numerous examples of industrial action on the part of Staffers. They have gone on strike, instituted lockdowns, worked-to-rule, engaged in slowdowns and set up overtime bans, as forms of industrial action (these will be revisited in the next section). These have all been reactions to their perceived mistreatment by Management. Staffers have protested against mass retrenchments, cost-cutting measures, reduction of pay, reduction of benefits, increased working hours, and many other Managerial decisions that they feel is unfair. Yet, these industrial actions have not always worked. More often than not, Staffers themselves are not united enough to fight against Management. American author Jack London, and a variety of other empirical examples, speak of "scabs", who are best described as Staffers who do not cooperate with the other Staffers during industrial action. Scabs often cross over to the side of Management and continue to work while their contemporaries are involved in industrial action. What scabs are effectively doing is that they're allowing Management to maintain productivity even in the thick of war. By feeding Management with the resources they desire, Management can continue to withstand the siege from the Staffers. When the protesting Staffers run out of resources, they will break the industrial action and either return to work, or leave the organization.

Scabs clearly demonstrate the individualized nature of the Staff contingent. Scabs continue working, despite knowing full well that their contemporaries are on industrial action, because they're acting on their sense of self-preservation. Being gainfully employed, receiving job satisfaction and making money all make more sense to the rational scab than fighting for a common good so that every Staffer's life can be made better. Why? The rational scab would weigh the options available to him:

First option: "Go on industrial action with the rest. Fight for our rights so that our lives will be better, yeah! There's a 50-50 chance of winning this one. Don't know how long it will take, but once it's over, we'll get our way, yeah! But in the meantime, I'd have to live without money. I got four kids, all hungry and one on the way. I'd have to stand out in the cold holding a picket. Winter's not a kind mistress in this part of the country. Yeah… that's kind of a bummer."

Second option: "Carry on working. I'll still have money, and maybe I can pick up some extra money doing overtime work to fill in for the guys who are picketing. I'll be warm in the workplace. I'll have access to bathroom facilities. Hmm… the second option sounds pretty good, doesn't it?"

## FIGHTING CAPABILITIES

Different warriors have different fighting capabilities. Archers, for example, are long-range fighters, who position themselves behind fortification or go on horseback to execute offense. Foot soldiers, for example, are in the frontlines, and engage in close combat. Elite squads, for example, try to sneak behind enemy lines and engage in stealthy tactics. In this same line of argument, Management and Staffers have different offensive strategies, different defenses and different ammunition.

At the outset, let's not pretend that Staff and Management are equals. They're not. Toe to toe, Staffers look like Gomer Pyle, while Managers look like Sergeant Carter. Gaww-lee, that's an apt comparison is it not? In countries where labor laws are more partial towards workers, such as Belgium, France and Sweden (see article by Eisenbrey), Gomer Pyle gets an extra bullet and a thicker protective vest against Management. However, in countries where labor laws are weak, and various forms of modern-day slavery exist, such as India, China and Pakistan (see article in *The Hindu*), Gomer Pyle gets a gag over his mouth and shackles on his feet. Despite the variable deviation between Staff and Management, we can still look at the fighting capabilities of Staffers and Managers separately.

Let's start with Staffers. Staffers have limited defense capabilities. They tend to be stronger in offense rather than in defense. Why is that? Well, firstly, Staffers can't defend themselves too well because they are not a united contingent, as has been discussed earlier. Staffers by and large tend to be individualized, seeking remuneration and satisfaction only for themselves. Another reason why Staffers cannot defend themselves all too well is that Staffers are constantly being evaluated against a performance benchmark by Management. Any deviation from that benchmark, and Staffers would have to justify their underperformance to Management. Accordingly, Staffers do not have a lot of defensive strategies on their part. Some defensive strategies include keeping silent in order to prevent themselves from being misunderstood, misquoted or misinterpreted, placing mirrors on their desks to prevent themselves from being spied on, and minimizing contact with Management. However, Staffers have a lot of offensive capabilities at their disposal. Staffer offensives can run the gamut from the light attacks, such as spreading gossip about a certain dislikeable colleague, to heavy attacks such as industrial action. Various tactics have been discussed in Chapter 1 regarding how one can maneuver around various types of colleagues. Some of these maneuvers are offensive, while others are defensive.

Comparatively, the Manager, on the other hand, is a warrior with a heavy set of defense and offense. Light defenses and attacks don't work so well for the Manager as warrior. Being vested with powers by the organization, Managers stand as defenders of the organization. They're like the Centurions we see in *Asterix* comics. On their own, they already possess a pretty solid shield. When they're in tortoise formation (tetsudo), they become impenetrable (to most, save for the Gauls). They will stand together to protect their entire contingent. Zigackly. Ferpectly right. For a more in-depth look at Roman military tactics, look up Cowen's and Rance's works.

Management is capable of defending each other, defending selected Staffers and defending the interests of the organization. The trust that has been given to Management to keep safe the name of the organization imbues them with heavy defense capabilities. Note, however, that the capabilities of individual Managers are not always equal to one another. Simulators, for example, are not as capable of defense as Artful Dodgers are. Simulators maintain a distance, and that distance serves as their shield. But Artful Dodgers defend by hiding and using information to their advantage. Once an opponent breaches the distance, a Simulator's defense is effectively broken, but Artful Dodgers can maintain defense all the way into a corner, and still may emerge victorious.

When Management attacks, Management attacks hard. Heavy artillery is the way that they go, because light firepower does not suit their warrior class. Recall earlier that Staffers can use a variety of light attacks. They could ostracize a common enemy. They could refuse to answer the requests for help by a certain colleague. They could use sarcasm and claim not to know any better. These don't really work for Management. Ostracizing a common enemy could work within the ranks of Management, but remember, the group preservation sentiments will always prevail. They should, would and could not refuse to answer the requests for help because they are held accountable for the deliverables by their Staffers. Well, they could always use sarcasm, but they cannot claim to not know the proper practices, procedures, policies and philosophy. So, what is this heavy firepower that we're talking about here? Management will use offensive techniques that involve reproducible evidence and noticeable behaviors. Reproducible evidence as opposed to hearsay, and noticeable behaviors as opposed to intentions. Notice that these heavy firepower items are very similar to the ones required by the judiciary for legal disputes. As defenders of the organization, Management technically have to uphold the legal contract that defines the employment in the organization. As has already been discussed, the idea of a social contract is often sold as the "glue" binding colleagues together in the workplace, while the legal contract is the one that often is resorted to in dealings between Managers and Staffers.

Where reproducible evidence and noticeable behaviors are lacking, what would Management use as offensive techniques? Management would then choose to use "passive offensive" techniques rather than "active offensive" techniques. In the language of behavioral psychology, instead of "positive punishment" (or, adding a negative stimulus), Management would prefer to use "negative punishment" (or, removing a positive stimulus). Knowing full well that individual Staffers seek to balance the effort they put in at work, with the returns and satisfaction they get from it, Management often use passive offensive techniques to set this balance off. With the balance being off-centre, Staffers will try to readjust their strategies to set the balance right again. Management can quite easily set the balance off by giving individual Staffers more work, or getting them to rework on a certain deliverable many times, causing a necessary increase in effort made. Another way would be to reduce the returns to Staffers through pay cuts or reduction of benefits. This directly affects the returns that Staffers get, causing their individual equations to fall off balance. Yet another way would be to reduce the satisfaction Staffers get from the job. An effective way that has been found to reduce Staffers' satisfaction is to reduce their workload. You read that right. Reduction of workload can be effective as a passive offensive technique, contrary to the opposite move of increasing workload, as has just been discussed. Reducing workload takes the joy one gets out of getting the job done, and would thus reduce the satisfaction one gets from the job overall. The discerning Manager would be quite careful in selecting the types of work to reduce, though. The most effective tactic, using this method, would be to reduce or take away the projects that the targeted Staffer feels most passionately about. This is based on the understanding that not all tasks at the workplace are enjoyable. Most Staffers feel passionately about certain tasks, tolerate other tasks, and hold yet other tasks in disdain. Reducing tasks which Staffers don't feel passionately about would be quite welcome to Staffers, as one would imagine!

Another offensive technique that individual Managers like to use is a parry-type technique known as "deflection". We know that Management's defensive capabilities way outstrip the defensive capabilities of Staff. Managers carry big shields, and shields are not just good for sheltering against attacks. They're also good for deflecting attacks to an unsuspecting victim. We've all seen how Captain America does it, haven't we? By tilting his shield to a sweet angle, the bullets flying towards him can be deflected towards other enemies elsewhere. When a Manager gets rained down from above, as mentioned earlier, he could either shelter his Staffers from the onslaught, or he could shape shift into another archetype. But what if he angled that shield ever so slightly downwards, and deflected the bullets from his superiors to his Staffers? Yup, that happens more often than we care for doesn't it? When orders from above come raining down, a lot of the times Managers pass those orders down to us without so much as an explanation for those orders. By deflecting those orders downward towards us, Managers are exercising a keen sense of self-preservation. We are made to obey and answer directly to those orders from above, while no harm goes to said Managers.

## MANAGER-STAFFER ALLIANCES

Now, I know some of us get along with our Managers. And we've also seen how some of our colleagues get along with certain Managers. Of course, there are also those of us who can't stand to even look at certain Managers, and some of us avoid Management like the plague. This section will be devoted to alliances between Managers and Staffers. We will discuss why alliances between Managers and Staffers exist, what some of these alliances are, and how we can maneuver around them.

First up, why do alliances between Managers and Staffers exist? Aren't Managers and Staffers polar opposites like the Capulets and Montagues? Or something more sinister like the Crips and Bloods? Well, yes, Managers and Staffers are diametrically opposed to each other, for various reasons. One, they have completely opposite interests of each other. Managers are interested in maximizing productivity from and minimizing returns to Staffers. Staffers are interested in maximizing individual remuneration and satisfaction while minimizing effort. Two, Management has been given the mandate to watch over and make sure Staff toe the line, while Staff have no such mandate in return over Management.

Now, some might say that Managers are sincere in wanting to offer a hand in friendship to Staffers. The more cynical of us might say that Managers are never sincere, and that they're just using us Staffers to promote their own agenda. To me, though, neither of these is completely true all the time. Managers and Staffers ally because it brings mutual benefit to both, a "symbiosis", using ecological terms. The relationship will only be maintained as long as the mutual benefit remains. Without that mutual benefit, there will be no alliance. For those of us who avoid Management like the plague, yup, you guessed it, we saw no reason for us to ally with Management. Of course, there were opportunities. We might have walked by the pantry and seen a Manager drinking coffee alone. We could have sat down beside him. We might have been taking a Number One in the bathroom, and seen a Manager at the adjacent urinal. We could have made small chat while our dragons drain themselves dry. But we didn't. Why? Because we saw that there would be little to gain from doing so. Some of us are really shy, and think that there would be too much cognitive load to pile up in order to gather our courage to make small talk. That cognitive load would have cost us a lot, and we probably couldn't see many perceivable benefits that would come from making that small talk. Hence, that gesture would have cost us a great deal of effort and little returns. No go. Some of us are really calculative. We didn't want to talk to that Manager simply because we didn't see explicitly how talking to him would bring us benefit. Would we get an edge up during the next promotion exercise? Maybe not. Well then, why bother talking to him in that case, eh?

Managers and Staffers can ally in a variety of ways. Firstly, the Manager and Staffer could be having an extra-work relationship. They could be having a romantic affair, or they could be part of the same old boys' network, or they could be having any other relationship that exists outside of formal work. Their alliance at work thus is an extension of their cordial relationship outside of work. Easy enough, that one. Secondly, Managers and Staffers could be allied for the purposes of succession management. That is to say, the Staffer is being groomed to be inducted into Management positions. This sort of alliance tends to be formal, but also long lasting, because grooming does take a while, and that relationship must be maintained at least until the newly inducted Manager stabilizes his position as a Manager. The groomer needs to groom that new Manager well. Why? Because there are sunk costs and transaction costs involved. Effort has been put in to identify the successor. That's not an easy task. It takes a whole lot of observation, a good track record of performance evaluation and justification. It could take hours, days even weeks of work to identify a successor. Earlier, under "Declaration of War" in Chapter 1, we discussed how to estimate the dollar value of sunk costs and transaction costs. Remember that? Now, if that new Manager is not able to perform his managerial duties well due to the lack of proper grooming, there will be transaction costs. There might be damage control that needs to be done, or he might even have to be replaced with another successor.

Let's see how much this could potentially cost a company shall we? So, John Doe, a senior Manager, decides that he needs to pass on his role to a junior Manager. He's planning on retiring in the next couple of years. John spends about 3 months observing all the eligible Managers he has under his care and identifies Jack Doe to take over his position. In total, he has spent about 80 hours looking through Jack's records, having casual chats with Jack, deliberating over Jack's suitability and such. That's 80 hours that could have been spent doing something more productive. At John's rank, 80 hours would probably cost the company, oh, I don't know, $1600, perhaps? Jack eventually gets appointed to take over John's position. John spends another 80 hours bringing Jack up to speed on what needs to be done and such. That's another $1600 lost from John, and you see, Jack needs to spend time picking up John's work too. That's $1600 lost from Jack. Just one succession has already cost the company $4800. In the event that Jack cannot perform in his new capacity, John needs to search for a new successor. Another $4800, likely.

On the part of the successor, he needs the groomer as much as the groomer needs him. Without getting the proper resources through grooming, he will not be able to perform his Managerial duties. Without allying with the groomer, he would be vulnerable to the dangers of being a Manager. A popular knowledge among militarists is that Military Officers who don their ranks proudly on their epaulettes are going to get sniped soon enough. This is because people in Managerial (or Military Officership) positions are often targeted by opponents. Opponents are aware that Managers possess a certain amount of power, and taking that power out of the equation would balance the battle back in the opponents' favor. Remember the part about group preservation among Management? A Manager who is left alone without the protection of his group is more likely than not, going to face the wrath of his enemies.

And then there are the more informal workplace alliances. These include how Brosses reach out to their Staffers, how Managers treat their project members nicely during the duration of said project, and also "Whisperer-Whisperee" relationships. These tend to be more fluid, in terms of needs. Brosses need Staffers to work harder, and thus try to reach out to them like a Bro. There isn't anything specific he'd like the Staffers to produce more of, but, you know, just work hard in general. Yeah, that'd be great. Managers also often tend to treat their project members way better during the duration of said project. These Managers need for that project to run smoothly and for every glitch to be patched up as soon as glitches are noticed. Thus, they're nicer during that duration. Same thing goes for Whisperer-Whisperee relationships. Whisperers need to feel that they're in touch with Management. Perhaps they're so righteous that they feel the compulsion to do the right thing every time. Perhaps they need the protection of Management. And Management needs them in turn. Management needs information from the grapevine, which they're not always privy to. Management needs opinions on what to make of various Staffers. In light of incomplete information, Management's best bet is to turn to a Whisperer.

## MANAGEMENT AS MEDIATOR

Oftentimes, in the drive to maximize individual remuneration and satisfaction, while minimizing effort, Staffers crash, boom and bang into each other. A variety of competitive relations can take place between Staffers, ranging from the "silent treatment" to outright aggression. During these times, Management might be called upon to mediate in order to untangle these competitive relations.

When Management mediates, they only have one intention in mind, that is, to ensure that productivity does not suffer because of the competitive relations. Don't be mistaken. Management doesn't give a cuff whether or not Staffers love each other. Our social relations at work are of little significance to them. The only thing Management is concerned about is that Staffers do not hate each other too much so as to reduce productivity. Management is also concerned that we do not love each other too much so as to reduce productivity. Which is why some organizations frown upon the idea of workplace romance (refer to Powell's article).

Bear in mind this Managerial Imperative when we're planning to complain to Management about another Staffer. Management will take action if and only if they see that taking action will result in higher productivity or lower remuneration. This is why, when complaining to Management, do not impose labels on the one we are complaining about. Calling another colleague "lazy" or "uncooperative" makes it look like we are the ones who are causing the productivity to dip, and Management would then blame us. Do state the actions of the one we are complaining about, along with the dates and the consequences. Remember that Management is a defense-heavy fighting class. Management does not have light offensive weapons in its arsenal as Staffers do. In order to use Management to fight battles for us, we need to feed them the only ammunition that can fit their weapons, that is, justifiable and reproducible actions. Not intentions. Not sarcasm. Not even body language.

Of course, Whisperers are exempt from these suggestions discussed above. Whisperers are already in alliance with Management, and so, have a different set of rules applying to the complaints they make. Why? Management trusts Whisperers to feed them with the information that is of interest to them. As such, complaints coming from Whisperers will be given a lot of attention to, because these complaints are trusted to be in the immediate interests of Management. As rational beings, Management's self-preservation mode suggests that they should pay close attention to complaints made by Whisperers.

What does this tell us? Don't expect Managers to be magnanimous. Don't expect Managers to play fair. Managers possess social, emotional and cognitive biases, just like every other human being. Certain Managers may have predispositions towards other ethnicities, religions, genders and sexualities. They may hold certain negative ideas which automatically put certain Staffers at a disadvantage in relation to them. Other Managers may have a chip on their shoulder and will thus act in an emotionally charged way. They may have had a bad day, or they may not be in the right mood to exercise non-emotional judgment. And then there are other Managers who just cannot understand us, for the life of them. One thing I've learnt about comparative human cognition is that we should never expect other people to have the same cognition as we do. The people that we meet in life have taken different routes to get to where they are. These different routes offer different experiences to these different people. Some people are lucky enough to get the scenic route, perhaps a walk in the park. By the time they get to where they are, they're still smiling and probably still think that clouds are made of white cotton candy. Others have had to jump through hoops of fire and climb over barbed wire to get to where they are. By the time they get to where they are, they're torn and tattered and probably don't trust their own shadows. Also, different people learn differently from their experiences. Some don't learn anything at all, and repeat their mistakes over and over again. Some learn quickly, and are able to apply those learnings to future scenarios. All these mean that different people have different cognitions, and we should not expect another person to completely understand us.

On top of these biases, Managers have been vested with power by the organization. Power can always be used and abused, and oftentimes, the line between "use" and "abuse" is unclear. Is a Manager using his power wisely if he puts in a recommendation to bring a friend into the organization? Is a Manager abusing his power absolutely if he puts in scathing remarks to get a Staffer fired? The point I am trying to make is, never ever put complete trust in a Manager who is involved in mediation between us and another colleague. Between their different biases and their different levels of power, Managers are always a grab bag. We never know what's inside, and frankly, we might be disappointed when we finally see what's in them.

What should we do if we are the ones being complained about, and Management is mediating between us and the complainant? Firstly, we should be aware that as soon as Management decides to mediate, they already think that productivity is taking a hit because of our actions. What this means is that it would be in our best interests to convince Management that productivity is still maintained at the level before the complaint was made. That would definitely satisfy the first level of thirst for Management. But you see, Management is always interested in maximizing productivity. Productivity is never enough. If there weren't labor laws, I bet you we all would be working our fingers to the bone, living in workers quarters and eating company-provided swill as our one square meal per day.

Secondly, we should be aware that when Management decides to mediate, they are ready for war. In other words, once Management invites us for a "chat", we can be sure that the drawbridge is up and the town gates are bolted. And we're just standing there with a slingshot in one hand and a pebble in the other. We suspect that there are archers waiting behind the arrowslits with bows drawn. We hear horses, which likely means that the cavalry is waiting behind the curtain walls, but we can't be sure. We smell tar and see smoke rising from the parapet, which could possibly mean that tar would be poured down through the murder holes. We're not going to go charging in, that's for sure. Not with a slingshot and one miserable pebble.

What can we do? Try to clear the fog of war and guess where their defenses and offenses are placed. Most likely, Management will place most of their defenses in front of the complainant, guessing that we will be defending ourselves by sending offensive attacks towards the complainant. We should not make our arguments by trying to pin the blame on the complainant, therefore, because we won't win. A better way would be to evaluate Management's ammunition. What sort of ammunition are they using? How much hurt can this ammunition do to us? Remember that Management can use all sorts of heavy artillery. They are likely first to draw us in with their observations and evidence of our behavior and our intent. These would then be compared to the company philosophy, policies, procedures and practices. At times, they might even compare our behaviors and intents to the company culture. They would then point out the gap between how we have behaved and what we have intended on one hand, and the proper or appropriate way, according to philosophy, policies, procedures, practices and/or culture.

They might say, for example: "I noticed that you haven't followed company policies properly. It states here under section something something paragraph something something that employees shall and must put on their nametags at all times".

Or how about his sweet ditty, "Here in this company we take pride in treating each other like family. We call each other by our first names. Your insistence on calling your direct Manager as "Ma'am" contradicts this very culture that we have worked so hard to cultivate".

When Management decides to attack, the best thing we can do is run. That pebble and slingshot doesn't stand a chance in hell against their infantry and cavalry. Being vested with the powers to defend the organization, Management is given the mandate to watch over Staffers and make them toe the line, but Staffers have no such reciprocal power over Management. Yeah yeah yeah there's that thing called 360-degree feedback but that's not a very popular system, perhaps because there's just too many variables to make it a sound method of evaluation (see Smither, London and Reilly's article). Added to that is the fact that many companies still resist adopting that idea, or adopt it half-heartedly (see Jackson's article in Forbes). At the end of the day, a very telling quote on the power that Management have over Staffers is the popular "people don't quit their jobs, they quit their Bosses". Managers can make or break our working experience. That's the bottom line.

# CHECKPOINT TWO

Here we are, at Checkpoint Two. Not all Bosses are horrible, but in the event that we do find something distasteful about our Managers, hey, try to fit them into the archetypes we have discussed here. There is "The Machiavellian Manager", "The Bross", "The Simulator" and "The Artful Dodger". No matter which archetype of Manager we might have, or even if they are genuinely interested in selling the idea of a workplace as family, all Managers share the same imperative of maximizing productivity from and minimizing remuneration to Staffers. The Managerial archetypes shown here are also neither exhaustive nor mutually exclusive. Managers can easily change from one archetype to another if they feel any sense of threat either from their own superiors, or from their subordinates. All this is a rational reaction to their perceptions of the Managerial Imperative.

Staff and Management are two different classes of fighters. For one, it is damn near impossible for Staffers to go up against Management. I guess that's why they call it a "Boss fight", huh? (Note to self: Stop the video game jokes. No one gets it). Management exhibits the Darwinian sense of group preservation. Managers are united in their mandate to represent the organization and to keep Staffers in line. Staffers, on the other hand, are in constant competition with each other for the same resources, and thus exhibit no such sentiments of group preservation. For another, Staffers have a limited range of defensive capabilities, but an entire arsenal of offensive weapons on hand. Just stop work. Simply refuse. That's an offensive, right there. Just tell the other Staffers about how bad Management is. That's an offensive, right there. Management, on the other hand, is a defense-heavy class. They are able to, and in most cases, will, defend the dignity of the organization, defend their own kind, and defend Staffers who they feel they need to defend. Offense-wise, though, they can only use heavy weaponry. They can't just initiate a light offensive the way Staffers can. It takes a bit of effort for Management to coil up for an attack. But when they attack, they hit hard.

We followed up by discussing alliances between Staffers and Managers. We discussed the idea of a congruence between the resource needs of Staffers, and Managers respectively, and the ability of each other to provide resources to each other, resulting in a symbiotic relationship. We ended the chapter by looking at the various instances in which Management can play a mediating role between Staffers. Some tips were given on how to make use Management as a mediator, and also how to counter when another colleague is using Management as a mediator against us.

This chapter also discussed the least popular people in the workplace, the Sandwiched Managers. Sandwiched Managers are the least popular people in the workplace because they're thought of as Managers by Staffers, and are treated as Staffers by higher Management. They're asked to take responsibility, and must subscribe to the Managerial Imperative. This makes Staffers wary of them, and they are thus treated like any other Manager would be. Yet, they are given little decision-making power, or power to influence change in their organizations. To higher Management, they're just trustworthy enough to have ownership over and take responsibility for projects, but they're not trustworthy enough to make decisions or influence change. Sandwiched Managers thus exist as a chimera of Management and Staff, with the worst characteristics of both species.

Management and Staff are indeed species which are diametrically opposed to each other, because both species are interested in taking away the very resources that the other needs. In the food chain, Managers are top-level predators, and

Staffers are bottom feeders. Because of this, Management is able to influence the direction, operation and culture of organizations. In the next chapter, we will be moving away from colleagues and Management, and looking at a premier battlefield in the workplace, namely, workplace theatrics. Break out the popcorn.

# CHAPTER 3: HOW TO SURVIVE ORGANIZATIONAL THEATRICS

So far, we have established quite a few binaries in this book. Maximization versus minimization. Management versus Staff. Offense versus defense. Here's another binary for us to consider: The workplace contains two kinds of work. There is real work, and then there's the theatrics.

Real work is the work that is done for the proper functioning of the organization. It is the core products and/or services that the organization produces and/or provides, and its main raison d'etre. Real work has timelines. Real work has a monetary value attached to it. Real work should be the only thing employees are concerned with. But it isn't.

Unfortunately, real work is often overshadowed by its nastier brother, organizational theatrics. "Organizational theatrics" I define here as that part of work that is done more for show than anything else. It has more value in its outlook rather than its content. This may sound familiar to scholars in the fields of cultural studies, postmodernism and symbolic interactionism. They'll know this as "simulacra", "impression management", "rhetoric", "semantics" and "discourse", among other terms that they use.

Marshall McLuhan wrote of the medium being the message. He was referring to how, when consumers consume media products, they place more importance on how those media products are being presented, rather than the actual content contained within. This makes sense also in interpersonal communications. The people who we speak to place a lot more importance on the tone of our voice and the words we choose rather than what we're trying to tell them (see Burgoon,

Guerrero and Floyd's book for a detailed explanation of such "non-verbal communication"). In the organizational context, theatrics are often paid more attention to, rather than the actual work. Theatrics can even sometimes represent the actual work that was done. Whether this representation is actually valid or not is questionable, though. Theatrics tend to get paid more attention to for several reasons. Firstly, theatrics are more public. Real work gets done at the desk, in the lab, in the ward or in the workshop. No one really sees how quickly we made that sale to a customer. No one really sees how beautifully we applied the paint job to that motorcycle. No one really hears the thanks we receive from that one patient who was so touched by our bedside manners. Theatrics, on the other hand, are easily seen by everyone all the time. Secondly, theatrics are louder, gaudier and more attractive. This suits the human brain, which is cognitively wired to be attracted to sensational information. Just think of the difference between facts and factoids. Facts are true pieces of information, while factoids are pieces of information which are not exactly true, but are easily believable because their sensationality appeals to the more basal side of our cognition. Information on things which excite us (such as sex and food) and things which scare us (such as danger and the paranormal) tend to be believed more easily than information on other topics because our instincts for pursuing pleasure and avoiding pain convince us that these pieces of information make sense and thus must be true. Same thing between professional wrestling and martial arts. Professional wrestling moves just look that much more painful and believable because effort is made to make each and every move look big, loud and impactful.

Some real examples from the organizational context, if you will. Ever notice how one takes extra care with one's appearance before meeting a client? The ladies may put on make-up and heels. The gentlemen may put on a coat and tie. Does appearance matter? I mean, we are meeting the client for a specific purpose, whether it be to deliver a deliverable or a sales pitch. Whether we dress up, or dress in rags, that content that we're delivering is still the same. So, again, should appearance matter? No. But does it? Yes. Well, that's one example of organizational theatrics. In this chapter, we will discuss more types of organizational theatrics.

But first, let's discuss why theatrics exist. On the part of Staffers, they are often aware that the evaluation of their individual performance at the workplace is not always a meritocratic enterprise. In many instances, different rules apply to different people. Many female Staffers are aware that dressing attractively at work may open up a new door of opportunities for them. Whether or not they agree with this phenomenon, or are even willing to partake in it for the sake of said opportunities is entirely their choice. Many Staffers of ethnic minority persuasion find that their ethnicities put them at a disadvantage as compared to Staffers from the majority ethnicity. This is because ethnic stereotypes persist, even in the workplace, making it hard for persons of different ethnicities to access the same playing field (we referred to this in the Introduction as a "glass ceiling"). In these instances, Staffers would turn to theatrics in order to minimize their disadvantage and maximize their opportunities. A female Staffer who decides to dress attractively could possibly be doing so to increase the opportunities available to her. An ethnic minority Staffer who plays down his ethnicity could possibly be doing so because he would like to be treated in the same way as ethnic majority Staffers.

In equally as many instances, Staffers are aware that their real work hardly ever speaks for itself. They know that they need to speak up for the work that they have done so that it is not glossed over or belittled by Management. Now, why does real work not speak for itself? Cognitively speaking, Management does not have the ability to remember all the work that all the

Staffers have been doing and how each and every task has contributed to the overall pooled output. Emotionally speaking, different Managers give different attention to different Staffers for different reasons. They could be sexually attracted to a particular Staffer, and thus unwittingly be paying a lot more attention to her. Behaviorally, they could disfavor another Staffer, and wish to downplay the effort he has put in. Managers are not always honorable in carrying out their duties as representatives of the organization, as we have discussed earlier under "Management as Mediator". As such, Staffers engage in theatrics in order to speak up for their own work. This, again, is a result of their desire to maximize individual remuneration and satisfaction while minimizing effort. One of these theatrical moves is to be regularly seen hard at work while Management is watching. Being seen acts as a stimulus, and when regularly seen, the stimulus maintains the conditions necessary for Management to register cognitively that the Staffer in question is indeed working hard. A furrowed brow, strategically timed as a Manager walks by the cubicle… a quickened step towards the photocopier when passing by a Manager's office… an email sent at midnight, with a Manager in the cc list… all send signals to Management that a Staffer is putting in a whole lot of effort. Another one of these theatrical moves is to deliberately make their work look much more important than it actually is. Staffers can choose to emphasize just how vital or crucial their work is to the larger output of the organization, even if what they did was not the lion's share of the work. Remember that example in Chapter 1 on how an Actor would snap photos of potential clients browsing at the company's roadshow booth and send those photos to Management? That Actor can follow up by insisting just how important those photographs were in ensuring the success of the roadshow. In that way, he is suggesting that his work should not be taken lightly. These theatrics cost a little bit extra effort, but, in the minds of Staffers who use them, the benefits outweigh the costs of putting in that extra effort.

Aside from Staff, Management also engages in theatrics. Management theatric, as compared to Staff theatric, is more of the "big-picture" variety, rather than at the individual level. Theatrical productions among Management are intended to showcase the health of the organization, that is, that the organization is doing well. It has long been an understanding among retail psychologists that consumers tend to buy more from a company that is doing well, rather than a company that is sickly. Money begets money, it seems. Retail psychologists have always recommended the practice of "facing", that is, to push products on shelves towards the front of the shelf rather than towards the back. This gives the impression that the supermarket is well-stocked, which will in turn invite more purchases (more is explained in Kit Yarrow's book *Decoding the New Consumer Mind*). In other types of organizations, Management tries to give this very impression of the good health of their organization for the very same reason. Clients will be more likely to spend more if they see that the organization is doing well. Shareholders will be more likely to purchase more stocks. Stakeholders will be more likely to pay attention to the organization. Aside from the outward-facing motivations, Management also has inward-facing motivations to use theatrics. Individual Managers are motivated to show to their superior Managers that the area under their management is well-taken care of. Remember we discussed the idea of different levels of focus for different levels of Management under "Caveat Lector" in Chapter 2? We discussed how the most junior level of Management looks over the practices, while the highest level of Management looks over the philosophy of the organization. Yup, that's what we're talking about here. Each level of Management doesn't want to give any reason to their superiors to suspect their commitment to organizational values and the trust vested in them. As such, they will explicitly demonstrate their commitment to managing their area of focus for the specific viewing of their superiors. Another inward-facing motivation on the part of Management is to show to Staff that the workplace is a paradise worth staying at. Why is that? So that productivity can be maximized, of course! Remember that Management is always interested in maximizing productivity (and simultaneously minimizing returns to Staffers). If Staffers develop the idea that the workplace is less than paradise, productivity can drop. For example, if Staffers get the idea that their work is not appreciated, they will reduce the effort they put in. Remember that Staffers are primarily interested in maximizing remuneration and satisfaction while minimizing effort. When they feel unappreciated, their satisfaction takes a hit. That is when they will reduce effort so as to balance the equation. A more extreme situation would be Staff resignations. Resignations are never one-off (see for example Smith's case study of doctors). Resignations beget resignations because resignations give a signal to the other employees that the organization in question is not worth staying at. Every succeeding resignation gives a stronger and stronger signal. In simple terms, the more employees quit, the more employees will quit.

Would organizations be concerned or nonchalant about resignations? What do you think? Organizations would really like to not give a cuff about resignations, and just employ new people to replace the ones who leave. They would really like to. But they can't (see Dewan's article in *Human Resources*). But it's not because they really care about you and me, though.

It's because resignations are costly on the part of the organization. Firstly, there will be a dip in productivity with every resignation because each resigned employee will have a handing-over period, where the outgoing employee will not be going full speed ahead at his tasks, but rather be slowing down so that the one taking over his tasks can catch up. Secondly, there will be costs involved in hiring a replacement. Money has to be spent to advertise for the vacancy. Time has to be taken to interview job applicants. Cognitive load has to be carried to consider carefully whether or not the chosen applicant would be able to perform to expectation. Time has to be spent to draw up a contract. Therefore, to maintain productivity at an acceptable level, the rational Manager therefore would try very hard to avoid resignations, or at the very least, keep employee turnover low.

Let's try to quickly calculate the amount of loss an organization faces when one employee resigns using some arbitrary numbers. We'll use that formula that we mentioned in Chapter 1. Let's look at John Doe. His average productivity can be pegged at the value of $5,000 per month, ceteris paribus. If he remains with the company, the company will be assured of $5,000. But John Doe has recently tendered his resignation. John Doe has to serve one month's notice. In that one month, John Doe will certainly not be producing close to $5,000 worth. He would be producing perhaps $2,500, half of that, because half his time will be spent handing over his outstanding work to the one taking over his role. The company will effectively lose $2,500.

Now, Jack Doe has been told to take over John Doe's role. Jack Doe usually brings in $5,000 on average too. But since he needs to spend time learning John Doe's work, he can only produce $2,500 in the current month. The company will lose another $2,500.

The company advertises for a replacement for John Doe. Applicants come and go, and the company spends a total of 10 hours interviewing applicants. The interview was conducted by two senior Managers. That's $200 worth of manpower cost that could be spent doing more productive things. Eventually, the company decides on one applicant to give the job to. That applicant needs to serve one month's notice to his current employer in order to leave. That's another $5,000 the company is not getting in John Doe's absence. In total, one resignation alone will cost the company $10,200, in this scenario. So, you can see why organizations are not too fond of resignations.

In the pages that follow, we will discuss a few more of the theatrics present in organizations. We will see the theatrics that Staffers employ for their individual rational benefit. We will also see the theatrics that Managers employ to demonstrate the health of the organization. We will see how these theatrics exist side-by-side with real work, and how theatrics often end up overshadowing the real work. Theatrics, while being less tangible and less measurable than real work, appeals to the rational side of Staff and Management alike.

## THE WORK PROCESS

Emile Durkheim wrote of a "division of labor" in modern societies where each individual's task is vital to the proper functioning of society. Everyone depends on each other to do their part, because one person's task is dependent on the performance of another person's task which in turn is dependent on the performance of yet another person's task and so on. Similarly, a division of labor is also present in organizations. Without the janitor, for example, employees won't have hygienic workspaces. Without hygienic workspaces, the production team cannot comfortably produce the goods. Without the production team producing the goods, marketers cannot take anything to market. With nothing to market, there won't be revenue. Without revenue, it would be damn near impossible to justify employing a janitor. Accordingly, various workplaces have adopted various formal and informal models of labor division so that inputs at every step of the work process can be given effectively, and transferred efficiently to the next person for his input at the next step of the work process. Several models of this have been noted:

The hierarchy model: The lower-level employees perform lower-level tasks, and the higher-level employees perform higher-level tasks. At an entertainment venue, for example, the busboys and clean-up crew do the lowest-level tasks, and get paid the lowest too, while the sound and lighting crew do a higher-level task than that, and the main performers perform the highest level task of all, that is, entertainment. Each task, as it goes up the hierarchy, builds up in value, with inputs adding value to the final product as it ascends the hierarchy.

The conveyor belt model: Each employee contributes one small part to form the larger whole. Typically seen in factories, the employee at the head of the conveyor belt lays down the base, which employees further down the belt add components to, and finally, the employee at the end of the belt closes the clasps on the final product. Each task performed has equal importance to the other tasks, and each task adds value to the final product by making it closer to being a complete whole.

The multi-functional model: All employees do all parts of the task from start to finish. An employee who finishes one part of the task simply takes on another part that has not yet been done. No employee's task is more important than the other. Quite typical of smaller organizations and start-ups, where the CEO of the organization can toggle between meeting clients and taking out the trash, the personal assistant can answer inquiries on the product, and the product developer can help schedule meetings for the CEO. This is a pretty communal model, with value being added laterally from everyone involved in the work process. It is not always easy to maintain this model. More often than not, organizations that grow in staff size and revenue shed this model and adopt the other models mentioned above.

Gerald Caiden has previously informed us of the "J-curve" of bureaucracy. What this refers to is that as companies grow larger, they will develop more policies and procedures, and with more policies and procedures come more inefficiency. The reason he posited was that rules beget rules. Rules, once made, attract more rules to manage the earlier rules. Eventually, rules get piled on top of more rules, and even after rules have become obsolete, they become so entrenched in the system that they become so hard to remove. It's like playing tetris. The lower blocks cannot be removed until the upper blocks are removed. And if the upper blocks are placed in an awkward position, it would be ridiculously hard to remove the lower blocks. Because of this, employees just follow those rules anyway, whether the latter makes sense or not. This behavioral trait is quite common among pubic serpents, I mean, pardon me, public servants.

Another manifestation of the J-curve that we could posit, following the central arguments in this book, is that as organizations grow in size, employees will show less and less of their full competence. Why?

Firstly, as organizations grow in size, employees realize that it becomes easier and easier to slip into the shadows. Procedures and policies bring along with them little nooks and crannies that employees can hide behind, and thus do not need to perform at their fullest. As the adage goes, one does not have to be good, one just has to be good enough. Not performing at the fullest is quite appealing to the rational employee. And why not? By reducing performance, employees are minimizing effort. They still get the same remuneration and satisfaction, but effort is reduced. The equation is balanced again.

Secondly, from a more Marxian perspective, as the organizations grows, the final product becomes less and less of a "species being". That means that employees have lesser sense of ownership over their work as the organization grows. While in small business units, one can actually see one's hard work coming to fruition, in a large organization, each and every employee who has direct input into the final product will amend the final product to his own style. The final product looks very different from how the employee who was at the beginning of the work process initially envisioned it. Imagine this scenario: While working in a small organization, John Doe was able to give candid suggestions to his Boss on the fly. Whatever idea he had, he'd just walk up to his Boss and speak his mind. His Boss would think it over, and either give him a green light to proceed or tell him to hold off for a bit. And then John goes over to a large organization. Every idea he has needs to be made through the proper channels. John has to speak to his Manager about it. With his Manager's blessing, John will then have to speak to that

Manager's Manager. With his Manager's Manager's blessing, John will then have to speak to that Manager's Manager's Manager. With his Manager's Manager's Manager's blessing.... I can go on forever, but you get the drift. Wait, I'm not done with the tale. So with every succeeding level John goes through, comments, inputs, further suggestions and amendments will be made to John's initial idea. Some Managers will not understand John's idea and ask for it to be simplified. Some Managers will want John to accommodate another segment of the clientele, and ask John to amend his idea. Some Managers will not agree with John's idea and insist John use theirs instead. John realizes that the final form of his idea looks nowhere near the initial idea he proposed. He agrees with some of the inputs made by the Managers because they made sense and helped him refine his ideas. But some of the suggestions he was made to incorporate was total bunk. He just had to incorporate them, just so that his idea would get through the "clearing chain" and see the light of day. John compares the satisfaction he got from working in the small organization to the satisfaction he got from working in the large organization. He has much less satisfaction working in the large organization. John's equation is unbalanced. He was seeking to maximize his satisfaction but it seems that it ain't gon happen. John would then seek to re-balance his equation. "Okay then," John says, "I'll just stop giving such complex ideas. Giving complex ideas had me jumping through hoops, and even then, the final form doesn't give me much satisfaction. I'd rather just give simple, cookie-cutter ideas. It will be less work for me."

Thirdly, employees are afraid that the reward for work well done is more work to be done. Bourree Lam makes this quite clear in a recent article in *The Atlantic*. Management tends to rely heavily on the competent ones, while allowing the less competent ones to take their time and work at their own comfortable pace and choose the kind of work they want to do. Why is this? On the part of Management, work needs to be done.

Yet, mistakes are always made in employing the wrong people (which happens more often than we think, according to Jeff Haden's article on *Inc.com*). And as organizations grow, it becomes harder and harder to fire employees. Rules have been set up to protect worker rights, and serious justification is needed to dismiss an underperforming employee. And thus, the Fumb Ducks become tolerated like a piece of furniture. Waste not, want not, right? What about the Actors? Well, they have their own way of showing Management that they're working their asses off, so Management thinks that they're pulling their weight. But we know that but they're not really doing much work. Yet, it is so very difficult to inform Management that the Actors are not really doing much. We're risking being thought of as the one causing trouble, instead of the other way around. This we discussed in Chapter 2 under "Management as Mediator". This results in Captains of Incompetence being tolerated, which is not to our liking at all.

But still... work needs to be done. So who is going to have to do the work? Why, the competent ones who have demonstrated ability and willingness to do them, of course! Management doesn't care. They only look at overall team productivity. So, suck it up, buddy. The competent ones always end up carrying the deadweight of the Captains of Incompetence. Now, do the competent employees want to let that happen? Hell, no! It goes against the very core of their rational judgments! By shouldering the effort of incompetent colleagues, the competent employees are putting in a lot of effort, more effort than will be rewarded through remuneration and satisfaction. And as rational beings, this will not be to their liking. The equation will be unbalanced, leaning on the costly side. The issue of unbalanced team effort will be further exacerbated when the competent employees realize that the work that they do to carry the weight of the Captains of Incompetence may end up being taken for granted.

But why would anyone take the work that a fellow colleague does for granted? Should they not remember it and appreciate it? They should, but they don't. This is because of several cognitive limitations that are inherent in human bounded rationality. Firstly, humans are programmed to cognitively give more credence to recent events. This is known as the "recency effect". Simply put, work that has just been done overshadows work that was done some time ago. This means that the work done by competent employees to pick up the slack for incompetent employees tends to fade away in organizational memory over time. Secondly, human cognition also features a "dependency effect". Political economists refer to this as a "moral hazard". What this refers to is that people tend to get used to certain actions, behaviors and favors done for them, and come to expect that those actions, behaviors and favors be done continually as a norm. People in organizations tend to become dependent when they see that there is no extra price to be paid for the actions, behaviors and favors undertaken. When they see that there is no need to reciprocate in terms of a return favor, they will tend to take the actions, behaviors and favors undertaken for them for granted, and will thus start depending on them. Thirdly, humans are also notorious for possessing a "negativity bias". It is so much easier for humans to remember what others did wrong, and forget what they did correctly. In the context of work, this suggests that anything that was done well by competent employees tends to be overshadowed by the errors they make. Errors tend to be amplified when made, while good work remains as muzak in the background. This idea has also been featured in Freudian psychoanalysis, where Sigmund Freud suggests that human cognition tends to downplay positive stimuli when in the presence of overwhelming negative stimuli. He argues that the ultimate state of bliss, therefore, is not where there is an abundance of positive stimuli, but where there is zero stimulus. In other words, it is the mental state of "death". This is why war veterans and rape victims tend to keep revisiting in their minds the traumatic episodes they went through, even though they are no longer in physical threat of those episodes. They're seeking to find happiness by deadening their senses and emotions (see Freud's discussion on the "death drive").

This is why rational employees will not show their full competence in organizations. For the ones who are comfortable just coasting along, such as the Dazy Logs, they'd hide in the shadows because they know that they won't be noticed as long as they keep under the radar. For the ones who are looking for satisfaction, they will quickly realize that their job satisfaction gets reduced as their organization grows. The final product becomes a watered down version of their initial vision, causing a lowered sense of ownership over the final product. For the ones who are aware of the effort they have to put in, they will be very wary of showing their full competence, lest they are made to carry the weight of the incompetents.

The work process in organizations, no matter what model is in use, will contain a healthy dose of both real work and theatrical work. The Actors will tend to use a helluva lot more theatrics than doing the actual work. The most sincere of employees (including some of the Non-Competitive Ones) will give their full effort to real work, and not indulge in theatrics. For the rest of us, we're always somewhere in between. True, we get paid to do work, and work we must, but many a time, theatrics are needed for us to survive. Firstly, our work doesn't always speak for itself. There is no point in doing a perfect job if no one knows that we're the ones who have been doing it diligently. In fact, our colleagues will tend to forget the past good work that we've done if they are not reminded of it. This is why we need to ensure our visibility in an organization. Make colleagues and Management notice the work that we have done. Tactfully, please. To announce our work loudly like a town crier would make us no better than an Actor. Secondly, we need to use theatrics to tamper our competence. Dangers await us if we were to show our full competence at work. Showing our full competence might just invite more work to be piled upon us. Colleagues and Management will tend to become dependent on the work that we did previously, and especially with incompetent colleagues in the mix, we're the ones who will get to do the work that needs to be done in the present and the future. Working hard and busting our asses off at work doesn't guarantee a clear career path in the organization. At all. Not by a long shot. Being identified as a defender of the organization's interests does. One needs to be the prized show horse in the stable, not the mule in the field, in order to have the Master's favor.

## WORK-LIFE BALANCE

Again, I reiterate one of the central points of this book: Management seeks to maximize productivity from and minimize remuneration to Staff. In a perfect bourgeoisie utopia, owners of means of production would simply hole up proletariat and get them to work all day with only enough time to eat, sleep and answer the call of nature. And that still happens in cities and countries where workers are desperate enough to agree to such inhumane working conditions. Reports are rife from towns in China, Pakistan and India, among others, where this still happens. But in many other parts of the world, especially developed countries, there is no such bourgeoisie utopia. The image of a Machiavellian Manager acting as a slave driver is not a popular image anymore. Rather, the image of a caring Manager (such as a Bross) in a family-friendly organization tends to prevail in developed countries.

In response to this new and improved image of the Manager, organizations have accordingly responded with policies on "work-life balance". "Work-life balance" policies seek to offer a friendly image of the company to employees and stakeholders, by suggesting that work isn't everything. Work-life balance policies thus include procedures to allow Staff to enjoy life, sometimes even seemingly at the expense of the company. "Blue skies" practices, which encourage staff to leave before the sun sets, seems to be antithetical to the drive to work beyond expectation. Compassionate leave, childcare leave, sick days without the need to show official medical certification, wellness disbursements and such are all procedures that fall under work-life balance policies. Each organization has its own way of promoting work-life balance.

Work-life balance policies look compassionate, at the outset. They're really made out to look like the organization is not only productivity-minded, but are also intent on enabling their employees to have a life outside work. Instead of making the employees churn out work like how organ monkeys churn out music, organizations are openly inviting employees to take a load off and enjoy life. Sounds good doesn't it?

Sounds good on the surface, and for much of the time, work-life balance policies have been working quite well. But don't be fooled though. Organizations aren't really interested in allowing employees to stop and smell the roses. What organizations are really doing here is trying to stimulate productivity. Yup, the Managerial Imperative remains.

You see, organizations have begun to understand that work can only increase productivity up to a certain point, after which more work from that point on only serves to decrease productivity. Why is that? Because employees are not machines, of course! Even machines need downtime and maintenance. Human employees are the same. This is where "life" comes in. Organizations have begun to understand that up to that point of inflection, giving a bit more emphasis to life might just actually increase productivity! And this is where organizations have started exploring policies on work-life balance, for the purposes of helping themselves increase their employees' productivity. Like cartoon villains rubbing their hands in glee at their brilliant plans, organizations are convinced that the yoga sesh every Wednesday at 1600 hours is sure to refresh and rejuvenate the employees such that they can come to the office on Thursday and work like the Duracell bunny. Excellent, excellent!

Yet, not every organization is convinced that adding more "life" to the mix can make employees more productive. This is because "life" is a qualitative consideration and organizations are not made to handle that sort of subjectivity. Now, if we were to tell organizations that "a $100 dollar increase in pay would necessarily increase $1,000 in productivity", that would be much more easily understood by organizations, but such a general category as "life" won't be so easily understood or agreed upon by all organizations. Look, "life" can mean a once-a-week yoga sesh, or "life" could also mean a paid vacation to the Bahamas twice a year. It is too qualitative a consideration, and organizations cannot be convinced that a good measure of "life" can make employees more productive. Organizations are unsure of how much "life" to give, and how much more can productivity increase with the provision of that measure of "life". This is why work-life balance policies in different organizations differ greatly. And this is also why some organizations don't even have work-life balance policies. Work-life is a theatric that is not easily understood by all organizations. It's like watching an avant-garde masculinist play on the struggles faced by gay disabled African-American chess players. It's not for everyone.

Hey, but here's a theatric that is indeed for everyone: "work-life integration"! "Work-life integration" is a philosophy that most, if not all, organizations can agree with, simply because it is more explicitly tied to productivity. How? "Work-life integration" attempts to be a modern avatar of the good old Confucian saying "find a job you love, and you never have to work a single day in your life". Essentially, work-life integration hopes to make work and life so seamless that employees do not feel that work is an activity that is separate from life. Work becomes life, and one would live work, just as naturally as one would live life. Quite a sell, isn't it? It looks like a great theatric at first glance. But this is where the Managerial Imperative comes in again.

"Work-life integration" is designed to increase productivity beyond that of "work-life balance". Organizations are interested in maximizing productivity. Productivity is never enough. Organizations seek to continually increase productivity more and more. Under the principle of "work-life balance", giving a good measure of "life" increases productivity doesn't it? So, how would organizations increase productivity beyond that? By giving more and more "life"? "No, that can't be", say organizations, "That doesn't make sense". Indeed, it sounds very much counter-intuitive. Work and life both take up time. And time for an employee is finite. There are only 24 hours in a day. That yoga sesh we spoke about earlier already takes up 1 hour. Should organizations have a 24-hour yoga sesh then, if they wanted to increase productivity more and more? Where would that leave time for work then? Very confusing, this "work-life balance" is to organizations. But "work-life integration" is so so so much easier to understand…

Let me repeat. "Work-life integration" aims for us to make work as part of our normal everyday lives. What's wrong with that? Let me give you a clue. Do you take care of yourself and your loved ones well? Do you try to give yourself and your loved ones a good life? Do you get paid to live? No.

But you get paid to work don't you? Now when work becomes life, do you still need to be paid? Aha…

Therein lies the secret to work-life integration. When work becomes life, employees work because they want to, and they don't ask for extra payment for it. What organizations aim to get is a motivated, hard-working employee who does his job and doesn't ask for more money for more effort rendered. By voluntarily working, and voluntarily not asking for more remuneration, organizations are continually maximizing productivity from and minimizing remuneration to employees.

Yup, "work-life integration" is about integrating work into life. Not the other way around, my friends. No organization will be keen on us walking into the office in bedroom slippers and watching the game with a beer in hand while a boardroom meeting is supposed to be going on. They'd be happy if we held teleconference calls on Sundays and worked on our laptops while the family barbecue is going on, but the other way around doesn't work for them. Why? Organizations don't really care about our lives. They care about productivity. The only reason they have to care about our lives is that our lives impact our productivity.

The best thing about "work-life integration" is that organizations need not come up with policies and procedures to bring it to light. Unlike "work-life balance" which requires organizations to set aside time and money to help employees enjoy that little bit of "life" among the hustle and bustle of everyday work, "work-life integration" only needs constant encouragement and motivational words by way of Management. In this manner, organizations are imposing on employees what Michel Foucault calls as "governmentality". "Governmentality" is the idea that powers-that-be instill into us ideas on how to conduct ourselves in the manner that they want us to. By instilling into us these ideas, we will begin to conduct ourselves in that way automatically, without the need for constant reminders, chastisement or punishment.

So the next time we go back to the office on a weekend just to finish up some unfinished reports, or we wake up at three o'clock in the morning just to telephone our Business Developer with a brilliant idea we have, we know we've contracted the "work-life integration" heebie-jeebies. The organization would be pleased. We've just voluntarily worked for no extra remuneration.

## ONE BIG HAPPY FAMILY

Another theatric of contemporary organizations is that of the workplace-as-family. Departing from the alienating workplaces of early industrialization (see Foster's book), contemporary workplaces hard-sell this idea of the workplace-as-family. Some workplaces still hold on to the traditional concept of workplace as primarily a place of business, no doubt, but there are many organizations that think that selling the workplace as a family is a much warmer rhetoric to employ rather than a place to just make money at.

Doesn't it just give us the warm fuzzies to be in a workplace that treats us as family members? I mean, I'd be happy to come to work every day seeing all the happy faces smiling back at me. It'd be like Seventh Heaven, wouldn't it?

Of course, at first glance, a workplace that treats employees like family members looks like a fantastic workplace to be a part of, but do you really think workplaces really care for us that much? Hell, no! They care about productivity. Workplaces have rationally calculated that by treating employees like family, they'd have a better chance at maximizing productivity and saving cost. The Managerial Imperative remains. So, how does selling the idea of the workplace-as-family help maximize productivity and minimize cost?

Firstly, with the workplace-as-family comes the rhetoric that family members will not be calculative with each other. As such, colleagues will not demand that favors be returned and ask for extra pay every time they work overtime. This helps organizations in the sense that they can save money on transactions between colleagues, as well as between Staff and Management. In an arms-length situation, we would ask for the exact remuneration for work rendered, right? Remember how we discussed the monetary equivalents of qualitative costs in Chapter 1 under "Declaration of War"? For each extra hour we work, we would ask to be paid our rate for one hour. That's in an arms-length transaction. In a more familial-like setting, we'd just write off that one hour as "good faith". That's in a nutshell what organizations want. They want us to give them "family discounts" on the amount of work that we do.

Secondly, with the workplace-as-family comes the rhetoric that family members will help each other out willingly and unconditionally. As such, colleagues will not think twice about standing in for each other at work, in the event that one of them cannot be present to undertake the task. There will be no return favor expected, because family members will unconditionally help each other. This helps organizations because all systems are always go! Imagine this: in a more transactionary organization, employees will not readily step up to bat for each other. They will ask "why me?... where is the person responsible for this?... can anyone else do it?" And if they are forced to stand in, they will do so grudgingly. They are also likely to ask for a return favor from the person who was absent. In the time that it takes to ask "why me?... where is the person responsible for this?... can anyone else do it?", minutes are lost, cognitive load is carried and effort is made. These all add to transaction costs, which the organization is not too fond of. Worse is if the resolution to these queries are so slow that it affects the work process or sales. Real dollars will be lost. Organizations sure as hell don't want that to happen. With a more familial organizational culture, there will be much lesser transaction and monetary costs with colleagues helping each other out willingly and unconditionally. The organization proceeds like a well-oiled machine.

Thirdly, with the workplace-as-family comes the rhetoric that family members will forgive and forget. Indiscretions appear at the workplace time and again. Some are deliberate, while some are not deliberate but are still offensive to others. Conflict will appear because colleagues are working in such close quarters with each other. This is even more so because colleagues in the workplace are fighting for that same set of resources. Now, conflicts have costs, as we discussed earlier under "Declaration of War" in Chapter 1. These costs, when borne by individual employees, are not an issue to organizations. For example, our organizations will be quite happy for us to take a taxi to work without us claiming for that transport cost. They will be quite happy also for us to use our mobile phones to call overseas without us claiming for that telecommunication cost. But when these costs are borne by the organization, that's when organizations become unhappy. Conflicts at the workplace do cost the organization. In the time that it takes to resolve a conflict, time is wasted. Effort is made to resolve it. Cognitive load is carried to understand each side of the conflict. All this costs productivity. When colleagues act like family and forgive and forget, conflicts will be downplayed greatly and resolved quickly. There will be no cost onto the organization. The organization is happy.

Fourthly, with the workplace-as-family theatric comes the rhetoric that family members will not keep secrets with each other. Information has a price. Knowledge is power. Many employees use information as resource at the workplace (see article by Fortado on how this happens). Information is traded for the purposes of getting advantage. Gossips act as dramatized pieces of information. Information is spread through the grapevine (see article by Burke and Wise for a deeper analysis on the office grapevine). Family members, though, do not keep secrets from each other right? There are no locked doors in households, right? No skeletons in the closet, right? At least that's what organizations would like employees to emulate. Of course this is a "simulacra", a copy without an original. Family members keep tons of secrets with each other, for various reasons. Some are ashamed of their past. Some are just protecting the innocence of the younger members. Households do have locked doors, as we all know. For a variety of reasons, again. We don't want to give the young ones a scare by walking in on us changing, do we? Or we might just need some private time to ourselves. And hell yes, there are skeletons in the closet in every family. Anyone who chooses not to believe so is in complete denial. We all live in society and we interact with others outside our family units. Those interactions have an impact on us, and may lead us to behave in ways that may not be approved by our family members. When these behaviors become skeletons, we put them in the closet to hide away and never be heard of again. So why would organizations want us to emulate this copy without an original? Because it is to their benefit, of course! How? Well, with the idea that colleagues should always be open with each other, organizations will be able to command and control the grapevine (according to Cathmoir, gaining control of the grapevine is one of the major victories of organizations). They will be able to manipulate information as a resource. So many battles throughout history have been about controlling channels of transportation and communication. By capturing a strategic route, or even better, a main supply route, an army can effectively set up siege (such as was done by Hitler's army in the Siege of Leningrad during World War II), cut off supplies (such as was done by the Syrian army to cut off reinforcements and supplies to the Islamic State in Iraq and Syria (ISIS) in 2014) and even create a chokepoint for the opponent (such as was done by William Wallace's army against the English army at the Battle of Stirling Bridge in 1297). (If that last name sounded familiar, think of blue war paint, men in kilts and the cry of "Freeedooommm!")

While this idea of the workplace-as-family works very well for the Management Imperative, workplaces aren't readily transformable into family units are they? One can be born into a family business. One can start a business with one's family members. But one cannot turn a business into a family, not without a whole lot of effort at least. Management, as the representatives of the interests of organizations, has tried to force fit this organizational square peg into the round hole of the family (sounds literally incestuous, I know). The result is often a "manufactured culture" of the family being forced onto employees at the workplace. Not every employee agrees with the theatric of the workplace-as-family. This is because of the issue of "trust" between colleagues. Now, as we have discussed earlier, Staffers are competitive beings, and compete with each other for the same existing set of resources. Each Staffer is primarily concerned with maximizing returns and satisfaction while simultaneously minimizing effort. Staffers exhibit a high level of individualism and almost no sense of group preservation. The only sense of "family" or group preservation occurs between Staffer cliques.

This issue of trust is the main issue that is preventing workplaces from ever completely achieving the workplace-as-family status. This is why the workplace-as-family is always a developmental process. The issue of trust, simply stated, is that Staffers do not trust each other to have their best interests at heart. Staffers are just not built that way. They are concerned with their maximizing their own remuneration and satisfaction while minimizing their effort. They just do not see the benefit of treating another colleague as family. More importantly, as stated in first-person perspective, "If I were to treat you as family, will you treat me as family too?" Staffers do not trust each other to reciprocate the courtesy of treating each other as family. If they were to be less calculative with their colleagues, just like how they are less calculative with their families, they are not sure if their colleagues would in return be less calculative with them as well. If they were to help out their colleagues willingly and unconditionally, they are not sure if their colleagues will also help them out willingly and unconditionally. If they were to forgive and forget their colleagues' indiscretions, they are not sure if their colleagues will also forgive and forget their own indiscretions. More importantly, they are also not sure if Management will be so kind as to forgive and forget their indiscretions. And finally, if they were to be completely open with their colleagues, they cannot be sure that these colleagues will not use that very information against them. Remember the power of Gossipmongers. Gossipmongers can take in any fact about their colleagues, add salt and pepper, then resend that information out into the grapevine. No one wants to be familial with a Gossipmonger.

In short, Staffers cannot trust each other to treat each other reciprocally. Reciprocity is indeed the expectation of the rational being. There are very few situations where reciprocity is not required. Firstly, it is where the parties involved do not exercise rationality. Parents, for example, do not expect their babies to reciprocate their affection because parenthood is not an immediately rational exercise. Parents are aware of the larger goal of "group preservation" and thus see their babies as extensions of their selves. One doesn't expect oneself to love oneself back as much as one loves oneself, does one? Unless, of course, one is a master debater or a champion in pocket billiards. Secondly, it is where the parties involved know that there will be reciprocity anyway, and as such learn to not outwardly expect it. For example, one friend tells another, "Hey, you don't have to be so calculative and pay me back for every coffee I buy you, you know". Implicit within this statement is the understanding that the friend in question reciprocates with another resource, such as a listening ear, business contacts or pays for the beers whenever they go to the local bar.

At the end of the day, each Staffer will be very hesitant to make the first move to recognize another Staffer as family because of this fear of the unknown and lack of trust. They are more likely to wait for other Staffers to make the first move. In the language of "game theory", Staffers are always "in zugzwang" when it comes to trusting each other. That is to say, they are in the constant state of remaining aloof, because making the first move would not be beneficial to them.

Nonetheless, organizations are quite intent on selling the idea of the workplace-as-family. They acknowledge that making the workplace into a family takes considerable effort, and requires constant cohesion-building activities. These include things such as Annual Dinner and Dance events, weekly lunches and office outings, among others. During these events, Management will be watching and trying to notice how their family-building project is going, and how much of it we are buying into. How should we react to this? We could always tell them directly (or sarcastically, whichever) that we're not interested in their family-building project, but this would just incur their wrath. Why? Because by not buying into the family theatric, we have just demonstrated that we're not team-players. It's a bit of circular logic there (if we don't accept the family theatric, we're not acting like family), but it kind of feeds upon itself, you know? Another reason is because by not buying into the family theatric, we are potentially going to cost them in lost productivity. If selling the workplace-as-family theatric helps organizations maximize productivity, not buying the workplace-as-family theatric denies them of that extra productivity. And trust me, they hate that. Anything that costs them in terms of productivity will not be taken lightly.

Instead of disagreeing with them, we could always pretend to agree with them, right? I mean, if the organization can stage a theatre, we could always stage a side-show, can't we? So how do we make believe that we agree with the workplace-as-family theatric? Firstly, smile a lot. A lot. Remember that Management cannot use whatever you are hiding behind that smile against you. They can only use what is acted out, said out, or recorded. Smiling gives you an alibi as well, with the other colleagues. Anyone who is asked will attest to you being happy during such company events. Secondly, when in conversation with others, always ask them about their lives. People love to talk about their lives. Parents love to talk about their kids. Old people love to talk about the war. Managers, on the other hand, love to talk about their achievements. Ask any Manager about his achievements at work. He'll talk your ear off like there's no tomorrow. There are some good reasons for asking people about their lives. For one, it avoids putting us in the spotlight. The attention is on them, not us. We avoid having to tell others about our lives, which others may judge. For another, it makes them feel good that they've shared the best parts about themselves. It's cathartic, like a really loud fart. They will take some time to recover from that fart, and won't be so quick to bother us. Optionally, we might find out something or other about them that we could use in the future. Sometimes, people do slip up and tell us things that they shouldn't. Even if they tell us the most politically correct things, we can always add salt and pepper to that information for use in an offense, if we need to. Finally, always have an exit plan. If the event has a definite end time, excuse ourselves immediately at the scheduled time, with the excuse of having another appointment. If the event does not have a definite end time, we need a socially-accepted excuse to leave. Ask a friend to call us when everyone is settled and no longer paying attention to us. Take that opportunity to leave. Or we could also pay attention to the others at the event. As soon as one person has to leave, take opportunity of that temporary break in the time-space continuum and leave too.

## JOB INTERVIEWS

Job interviews are a prime venue where workplace theatrics take place. Both the job applicant and the interviewer want to put their best feet forward. It's much like a first date where we pay attention to even the minutest details in order to send a positive message to our date. Advice is abound on how job applicants should dress and talk during a job interview. This includes dressing sharply in appropriate office attire, not saying anything nasty about our past workplaces, and giving a firm handshake. All these actions are indeed methods of impression management, which, as we have discussed, are a form of theatrics.

On the part of interviewers, theatrics do exist as well. Interviewers will do their utmost to personify the needs of the job. If the labor market is tight, or the job is very demanding, interviewers will take on a rather tough persona to reflect the toughness of the context. If the organization is desperate to recruit, we can be quite sure the interviewer will be quite cordial. We have discussed something similar in Chapter 2, when we said that Machiavellian Managers tended to be predominant in tight labor markets and demanding jobs, while Brosses tended to be predominant in labor markets where there is an abundance of demand for labor. Interviewers will also be inclined to paint as best as possible a picture of the job scope and the organization. At times, during this theatrical process, some information might get lost in translation. In other words, the obsession with impression management during job interviews leads the job applicant to give off signals which is incongruent with the vital information he needs to consider taking up the job he applied for, and similarly, the obsession with impression management leads the interviewer to give off signals which is incongruent with the information he needs to consider whether or not to offer the applicant the job. So, what information would both the job applicant and interviewer need to make an informed decision?

What the job applicant needs to find out most is whether or not he can have more satisfaction, and/or more remuneration with less effort than he put in in his previous workplace. In other words, he wants to know if he can shift the equation to lean towards less effort, and more satisfaction and remuneration. This happens for both push factors away from an organization, as well as pull factors towards a new organization. Let me demonstrate.

John Doe works in XXX Inc. Despite being trained as an engineer, he's made to fetch coffee and bagels for his Managers, all day, errday. Satisfaction = low. He's paid peanuts, because, hey, he only has to fetch coffee and bagels, they say. Remuneration = low. Where do the coffee and bagels come from? He has to cycle halfway across town to a Mom-and-Pop diner to pick up the coffee and bagels twice a day because his Managers are fond of the coffee and bagels from that diner. Effort = high. John's equation is unbalanced, and not in a good way. That's the push factor. Bam.

John notices that YYY Inc. has an opening. An engineering position. Hopeful for an increase in satisfaction. Pay will be pegged to market rate for engineers. Hopeful for an increase in remuneration. Will be stationed at client's site, near to his home. Hopeful for a decrease in effort. John hopes that this job at YYY Inc. can bring back his equation to balance. And even better, maybe even tipping over to the side of remuneration and satisfaction outweighing effort.

However, at a job interview, the applicant doesn't give signals pertaining to satisfaction, remuneration and effort. Rather, the applicant gives the impression that he is willing to work hard, that he had a good track record, that he is willing to be part of a team, and that he has good knowledge of the company's reputation, philosophy, products and services. Those signals have nothing to do with satisfaction, remuneration and effort, do they?

On the part of the interviewer, what does the interviewer really want to know? He wants to know about how productive this job applicant is going to be. He already knows how much remuneration this applicant wants. It's usually quite clearly displayed on resumes and job application forms. In order to assess the applicant's potential productivity, he will need to know how well the applicant fits into the job. Will he be able to perform the actual tasks assigned to him? The interviewer needs to avoid the applicant turning into a Fumb Duck once assigned to work on tasks, you see. Then, the interviewer also needs to assess the applicant's fit into the organization. An organization that serves lewd, crude and tattooed customers (such as a biker's bar) won't exactly take too well to a meek, church-going, librarian-type girl applying for the bartender position, would it? More on organizational fit will be discussed under the section of "Diversity" later on in this chapter. The interviewer also has to assess the applicant's potential for movement in the organization. Employees often have to move horizontally and rotated to others jobs, or concentrically, with an expansion of their job scope, and sometimes vertically, when they get promoted to a higher rank. It is dangerous for an organization to hire someone who cannot be moved to other parts of the organization. Why? Because work requirements change in organizations. Sometimes, these changes are brought about by changes in demand from clients. Sometimes, these changes are brought about by changes in the direction from higher Management. Whatever it might be, task priorities and core businesses change. Having an employee who is unwilling to respond to such changes will negatively affect an organization's productivity.

But, during a job interview, the interview doesn't give signals pertaining to productivity. Rather, the interviewer gives the impression that the job that is being applied for is good, that the organization that is being applied to is great, that the organization supports work-life balance, that the organization is family-oriented, and that the organization supports diversity yadda friggin' yadda. None of these are going to be able to tell the interviewer anything about the applicant's potential productivity are they?

If we ever do get a chance to interview a job applicant, I would urge us to resist the urge to engage in theatrics. This is quite antithetical to our intuitive reaction of putting on theatrics as mentioned above, but I would argue that dispensing with theatrics is the more rational thing to do. Why should we dispense with the theatrics?

Firstly, this person might end up as our colleague in the future. Being concerned with theatrics might cause us to wrongly evaluate the application. An incorrect evaluation can have dire consequences on us. We might end up with a difficult colleague to work with, and worse, we might have to carry his weight while he happily draws a fat paycheck. Yes. Nobody wants to work with a Captain of Incompetence. Not unless one is an especially forgiving sort of fella.

Secondly, we should really put effort into this task of interviewing because Management has not made up their minds about this new person yet. In many instances, it would be very difficult to change Management's mind about a certain colleague, once their minds are made up. This is especially so for colleagues who are allied with Management (such as

"Whisperers"), and the ones who Management has decided to protect. Since no Manager has made up his mind about this new person yet, we have fair ground to assess the job applicant and make our recommendations without the need for theatrics.

Consequently, what questions should we ask without resorting to theatrics? Firstly, we should directly ask questions that concern the job scope that he will be undertaking. Assess his ability and/or willingness to perform such tasks and his willingness to undertake job rotation in the future. If he will be assisting us and our team, find out how soon he can hit the ground running. We could always use an extra pair of hands, and the sooner we get that help, the better. Finding out his willingness to perform such tasks saves us the hassle of finding out that he is not keen on certain aspects of the task, and also saves us the hassle of trying to convince him that he should take on these aspects with pride (I barf at the thought of having to say that). If the job requires, for example, him to do some tasks that not many people like doing, make it known and get his concurrence on the undertaking of those tasks. Not everyone likes to clean out the bathroom or to stand on the corner with a sandwich board. Without getting his concurrence on such tasks that might be perceived by many as being low in satisfaction, we are risking several things. Firstly, we are risking resistance on his part. He might outrightly refuse to do such tasks, leaving us hanging. We might end up having to do those tasks ourselves, if push comes to shove. Secondly, we are risking a negative impact on his level of satisfaction. Some people don't mind doing menial tasks, while others do. A colleague who is made to do a task that does not bring him satisfaction will not be motivated to carry on with the other tasks in the job scope. Thirdly, we are risking a job done poorly. When a task is done grudgingly, chances are, the task will not be done satisfactorily. There will just be cursory effort made, causing a final product of poor quality. At times, it might even need to be redone, which, as we all know, is really painful.

We should also find out his willingness to undertake job rotation. The last thing we want is a colleague who wants to stay put in his position until retirement, and not be moved to another project that requires doing. Manpower needs to be reorganized and redistributed according to the needs of the organization. I have heard of an instance where one employee absolutely insists that she wants to do one particular project and that one particular project only. She insisted that if no such project exists, she would like to be kept on the payroll for an indefinite period of time until such a time when such a project resurfaces. Believe it or not, some folks have major cajones and extra thick skin.

Secondly, we should ask the applicant questions that address his fit into the culture of the organization. As we have mentioned throughout this book, a congruence, or fit between the components of an organization ensures that the resources required are met. This creates ecological sustainability and stability in the system. An applicant who does not fit into the culture of the organization might suffer from anomie while he adjusts to the new culture, and possible alienation from the task and his colleagues. When this happens, not only is he not getting the resources he needs from the organization, he is also not giving back the set of resources that the organization requires. The organization will collectively be a more stable ecosystem if they were to exist without him. One good way to ask questions about the fit of the organization is to paint a picture of the philosophy, policies, procedures and practices of the organization and get his opinions on it. Describe the most common tasks required of staffers, as well as how these tasks are performed, the logic behind having to do these tasks, and the way the organization envisions their own products and services. All organizations have unique permutations of these four elements. Even organizations in the same industry will have different permutations. Some recruitment agencies, for example, prefer fast turnovers and as such, focus on the lower-ranking personnel in fast moving industries such as retail and construction. Other recruitment agencies, on the other hand, prefer a more boutique approach, and as such, focus on sourcing higher-ranking candidates for more "classic" industries such as law and engineering.

A large body of organizational literature suggests that an employee's experience counts for a lot in an organization, and sometimes even more than his formal qualifications. We should be careful how we approach a person's experience though, because his experience may not fit with the intended job description. Sometimes, an applicant's experience may not be easily translatable to the new job description. As they say, different pond, different fish. A person may have vast experience in a certain industry, but when he is brought into a new organization, he comes into contact with things which are new and alien to him. He would have to firstly adjust to the organizational culture. Even within the same industry, organizations differ in culture. KFC and McDonald's have different organizational cultures, as do Sears, Walmart and Target. He would then have to adapt his experience to the philosophy, procedures, policies and practices of the new organization. The people in the new organization would also need to be open to learning from his experience. Without this latter point, there would be no use for his experience in that new organization.

John Doe is a business developer. He was brought in to YYY Inc. because of his experience. As soon as John comes in, John notices that the business development in YYY Inc. is done by the product development team. "That ain't right", thought John. Product developers are not the best persons to sell the product.

They know it in and out. They know its flaws too well. They know its technical specifications. But they don't know how the target audience sees it. The target audience may not see it from a technical point of view. They make not even notice the flaws in it, because they use the product for certain needs only. So John tries to suggest to YYY Inc. that business development and product development should not be one and the same. The organization refuses to listen. They are adamant that the best persons to sell the product are the ones who developed the product themselves. It is their philosophy, they insist, to be self-sustaining. It gives character, they continue. And character is forged in fire, they continue. Having had enough of cliched motherhood statements, John shows them examples of how having a separate business development unit can help improve sales. "A business developer is there at the beginning of the sales and continues to provide after-sales service," says John. YYY Inc. is not interested in this idea. "It's just not the way we do things around here," the senior Manager says. John's experience counts for bunk.

At other times, an applicant's experience may actually be more than the job requires. In this instance, the applicant may get too ambitious beyond his station, which might incur the wrath of colleagues and Management alike. We have established that each organization has its own core business, stemming from its philosophy, policies, procedures and practices. Expanding outside of that core business is not always easy, because it takes Management decision and support from Staff. Many a time, when an outsider is brought into an organization, however, his experience will be vastly different from the philosophy, policies, procedures and practices of that new organization. As an outsider, he will be able to see the gaps in that new organization. He will be able to see flaws which cannot be seen from within. He will also be able to suggest new ways of expanding outside that core business. Yet, that core business is often a "comfort zone" for the Management and Staff of that new organization. They would prefer to stick to the usual ways of doing things. To Management, "if it ain't broke, why fix it?" The tried-and-tested way of conducting the core business has proven to be productive in the eyes of Management. Why risk a dip in productivity by doing something different then? To Staff, the usual ways of doing things already have a balanced equation. The remuneration and satisfaction is balanced with the effort made. New ways of doing things may not ensure that the equation will be balanced. Staffers are unsure as to whether an expansion away from the usual core business will bring about more remuneration and satisfaction. But it sure will bring about more effort, because effort has to be spent to learn from that new guy's experience. This is where the new guy risks incurring the wrath of colleagues and Management with his ambitious ideas.

Another body of organizational literature suggests that interviewers should evaluate the potential of job applicants for future growth. There is definitely some truth to that, but as employees of the organization, evaluating the potential of a job applicant does not help us one bit. Firstly, we are not kingmakers. Even if the job applicant does have potential, we cannot help him realize that potential by catapulting him to a high rank, can we? Secondly, as rational beings, evaluating an applicant's potential does not help us much at all. As mentioned above, we need the applicant to work on with us, and to execute tasks within our foci. Evaluating an applicant's potential looks beyond this foci, and thus does not help us.

## GIVING SUGGESTIONS

Whatever the work process may be, many organizations have instituted systems of feedback and suggestions. These have ranged from the informal, regular requests for suggestions at every point throughout the work process, to more formal systems where suggestions are encouraged through rewards for each suggestion made or implemented. There are some noble intentions of asking for suggestions. Firstly, asking for suggestions gives employees a certain ownership over the work process. Ownership encourages employees to think of the final work product to be a part of his "species being", to use Marxian terminology. The feeling of ownership gives employees incentive to continually put in effort for future work, so as to continually feel like they own a part of the organization. Secondly, suggestions can bring about fresh ideas that would not be normally surfaced in the regular work process. Employees working on certain projects may be too close to the project to see its flaws, and someone further away may be able to see the project with fresh eyes. This is where organizations such as 3M see the value in their "15% time rule", where employees can spend 15% of the available time in a work week working on something that is completely unrelated to their assigned tasks.

These noble intentions, however, are often hijacked by theatrics. These theatrics are the result of both Staffers' and Managers' rational intentions. In some cases, the giving of suggestions becomes a Commons where everyone wants to have a share. This is usually the case for projects where the leadership of the project is not clearly defined, causing almost everyone to want to have a stake in it. This situation is called the situation of having "too many Indian chiefs". Another similar adage would be "too many cooks spoil the broth". The final product of such a project often looks quite ugly, if all the suggestions made were to be given equal attention and consideration. In other cases, suggestions given are evaluated ad hominem, and ranked according to the suggester's position in the organizational hierarchy. In other words, suggestions given by those of higher rank are given more consideration that those of lower rank. To adapt from Orwell, "all suggestions are equal, but some suggestions are more equal than others". In yet other cases, suggestions are asked only as lip service. Management is not really interested in suggestions from others, because they are already convinced of their intentions and further actions. Whether or not these intentions and further actions are smart ones, is up for debate. In combination, therefore, inputs and suggestions from Staffers are often solicited, but not desired. Staffers who are caught in this position are sometimes aware that they are required to give suggestions, but are also aware that their suggestions are most likely not going to be accepted.

If we ever get caught in such a position where theatrics shroud the suggestion process, exercise our rational judgments. It would be fantastic if we could offer creative suggestions and consequently have ownership over the projects, products or services that our organizations provide. That would indeed allow us to maximize our satisfaction from our jobs. However, in the absence of the potential for maximizing benefits, our rational judgment can, and will try to minimize the cost borne by us instead. In short, use our own theatrics to reply to the organization's theatrics. One way to give suggestions, when we know that suggestions are ranked according to the suggester's rank is to give only the kind of suggestions that Management wants to hear (remember, Actors are really good at doing this). The reason for this is that any other suggestion, other than the suggestions given by Management, will have a low likelihood of being accepted. By giving suggestions which Management wants to hear, we are reducing our effort by not putting in too much thinking and hope into the suggestions we give. Another way to give suggestions, in the spirit of minimizing effort, is to seriously consider the amount of extra work we need to do in the event that our suggestion gets taken up. Now, if the extra work that we need to do following our suggestion brings us remuneration and satisfaction, it's quite welcome, isn't it? But if the extra work that needs to be done will be tedious, or if we have to do the legwork just to have its ownership transferred to another person later, it would be foolhardy for us to make such a suggestion. If we are faced with such instances, make suggestions that already build upon or overlap with the work that we have already done. That way, the effort made to follow up with that suggestion would not be overwhelming. The last thing we want is overwhelming work that doesn't satisfy us or give us the returns we desire.

# DIVERSITY

Another popular contemporary theatric today is that of "diversity". All of a sudden, every organization wants to jump on the diversity bandwagon. No, I'm not talking about "equal employment" policies which give disadvantaged people (minority ethnicities, female gender, homosexuals, etc.) as equal a chance as any other person. That's a good thing. The color of a person's skin, their gender identity and their sexual preference has absolutely no bearing on their ability to think, communicate and perform work tasks. In fact, many countries in the industrialized world now have equal employment policies stemming from earlier affirmative action policies that seek to remove barriers of disadvantage.

I'm talking about "diversity in thought", "diversity of skills and knowledge" and "diversity in attitude". Many companies now are spouting their embrace of such diversity. They're employing people from various educational qualifications and prior job experiences just so that they can fly the flag of diversity. A lot of the time, this theatric fails miserably.

Why is that? Organizations that jump on the diversity bandwagon often do so without doing a "needs analysis". A "needs analysis" is an analysis of the current products, services and market presence of a certain organization, as compared to where it wants to be in the foreseeable future. The gap between where it sees itself, and where it currently stands, reflects the "needs" of that organization. To fill those needs, it can add do a whole bunch of things. It can build capabilities from within, which can take quite a long time, or it can bring in new blood, or it can change its philosophy, policies, procedures and practices. Lots of things it can do.

Now, diversity is one of the ways to address these needs, but what organizations fail to realize is that diversity can actually backfire for a couple of reasons. Firstly, diversity will backfire if there is a disjuncture between the needs and the contribution of the diverse elements brought in. The diverse elements will not be able to contribute to their maximum capacity because the needs of the organization differ from what they can contribute. The organization, as ecological niche, will not be able to support the growth of these employees, and these employees in turn, will not be able to reap the resources they desire from the organization. Simple example. You own an entertainment company. You want to move into the wedding singers market. You go out and employ clowns, rodeo cowboys and porn stars. Missing the point, much? Some organizations employ all sorts of people from all sorts of backgrounds without thinking about how exactly these people are going to contribute to the organization.

Secondly, diversity will backfire if there is resistance to said diversity. Resistance can come from a whole bunch of places. Under the section of "Fighting Capabilities", we have discussed how Staffers can use a whole range of light and heavy weaponry, and how Management can generally use only heavy artillery. Staffers can very well resist diversity. They could spread gossip about the new divergent employee brought in, or they could openly ostracize him. They could even raise their "concerns" about how he deviates from the rest of them to Management. Management could resist by using their power to place him in positions where he cannot use his diverse thought, knowledge or skills to make any change. And why would they do this? Because as an organization grows, it develops a culture. Within this culture are the norms, attitudes, beliefs and practices that almost everyone in that organization has grown to accept. The introduction of a diverse element upsets this culture. Imagine a foreign object in your body such as a splinter or a piercing. Your body will try to reject it. The organization will firstly try to incorporate this diverse being into the culture by getting him to agree with the norms, attitudes, beliefs and practices. In doing so, the diversity is effectively rejected by the organization because it has been converted into the mainstream. In the event that the diverse being cannot be tamed, the organizational culture will reject him in the ways that have been described above.

Another resistor to change is the actual organizational structure itself. As we have discussed earlier, organizations tend to put on rules as they grow bigger. Rules beget rules and pretty soon, rules form what Max Weber calls as the "iron cage". The "iron cage", once taken shape, dictates the accepted and approved ways of behavior within the organization. Any divergence from that will be met with chastisement and disfavor. The iron cage thus is a form of passive resistance to divergence. Divergents will be made to maneuver around the organizational iron cage just like every other employee is doing. This prevents them from applying their diversities of thought, knowledge, skills and attitude.

Let's ask ourselves: How divergent do we think we are in our organizations? Do we have a special set of skills and/or knowledge base that is different from the skills and knowledge possessed by the other colleagues? If so, evaluate the amount of contribution we can make to the work process and the final output. Can we put these special skills and/or knowledge base of ours to good use? We can only do so if our organizations have made arrangements in the work process such that our skills and knowledge can prove to be useful. If our organizations still wish to retain the tried-and-tested ways of conducting business, our divergent skills and knowledge may turn out to be useless after all.

Are we divergent in terms of thought and attitude? We potentially may run into trouble with the colleagues and Management if our divergence is viewed as dissidence and deviance. Different organizational cultures have different degrees of tolerance for divergence. Some cultures are not very tolerant, and require all employees of the organization to look the same, sound the same, speak the same and walk the same as each other. Other cultures are more tolerant, and have guiding principles instead of strict requirements to follow.

John Doe, for example, began working for XXX Inc. quite recently. He notices that everyone leaves for lunch at noon sharp. He also notices that no one makes small talk in the office. Small talk is only made during lunch. John notices that the company-issued windbreaker was dual-colored and can be worn inside out or outside in. It was red on one side and black on the other. John notices that everyone in XXX Inc. wore the red part inside and the black part outside. Finding that a little peculiar, John inquired with a colleague as to why no one thought of wearing the red part outside and the black part inside. His colleague replied, "Why be different? Isn't it good to be the same as everyone else?" XXX Inc. is a prime example of an organization whose culture has little tolerance for divergence.

Jack Doe works for YYY Inc. His colleagues wear what they want to the office. They come in at staggered times. They leave for lunch at staggered times too. In the afternoons, they sometimes even break out the nerf guns and lightsabers for a battle. Nobody really cares for being the same as everybody else. The only thing they're bothered with is being present during meetings and delivering the deliverables as scheduled. YYY Inc. certainly has a more tolerant culture than XXX Inc.

If we were to find ourselves in a less tolerant organizational culture, chances are, our divergence will get viewed as deviance.

This is because the strict guidelines of that culture would see to it that any divergence necessarily violates the very principles of that culture. Worse still if we're trying to put our divergence to good use by suggesting new ways to think and new ways to view work processes and core products/services. That would be construed as dissidence because the very action of trying to suggest something different is a threat to the very existence of that culture. This is when we will face major resistance to our divergence. Remember, threats are never taken lightly by the Darwininan organization. Organizations seek to maintain their existence, and will battle anything that poses a threat to it.

If we were to find ourselves in a less tolerant organizational culture, do not exercise divergence. In fact, try our bestest to hide it, and blend in with the rest. We cannot and should not introduce change in such an organizational culture. We can only go along with the change that occurs from within that culture. Whether or not that change is in the same direction as our diverse thoughts and attitudes, no one can be sure. Our divergence, in this instance, may end up being the appendix. It's there, but it's useless.

## CHECKPOINT 3

This chapter was all about organizational theatrics. We started off this chapter by discussing what organizational theatrics are, and why they exist. We found out that both Staff and Management engage in theatrics, because real work in and of itself just does not cut it. As examples of organizational theatrics, we first looked at the work process. We found out that there were various models of work process from the inception to the fruition of the product or service. We also found out that certain work processes are more suited to larger organizations, and other work processes are more suited to smaller organizations. We also found out how employees tend to give less and less inputs as their organizations grow in size, for a variety of reasons.

Another workplace theatric that we looked at was the idea of a work-life balance. Now, granted that there are still many organizations that do not care much for work-life balance, however, work-life balance has been an increasingly accepted policy in many other organizations, as the "life" portion is seen to contribute quite effectively to the productivity drive of the Managerial Imperative. An investment in "life" is thus seen as a contributor to higher productivity returns. To further increase productivity and reduce remunerations, a more recent policy direction is that of "work-life integration". Work-life integration essentially sees no investment in the "life" portion. Rather, it professes that the "work" portion be given as important a treatment as the "life" portion. By selling this theatric, Management is essentially getting Staffers to engage in work with no extra remuneration. Ka-ching!

The work-place-as-family rhetoric is a really popular theatric in organizations. It works wonders for the Managerial Imperative because by treating the workplace like a family, Management is able to overcome many of the costs associated with having a primarily transactional workplace. And in doing so, productivity is also increased without the need for extra remuneration. However, we also found out that workplaces can never completely achieve the status of being a family because, unlike biological families, workplace "families" face a constant issue of trust. One can always make the first move to trust another colleague, but one can never be truly sure that the trust will be reciprocated. Hence, there is that stalemate where no employee is willing to trust another colleague completely as family members quite readily would.

The job interview is another popular workplace theatric that was discussed above. Both the interviewee and interviewer wish to put their best feet forward, as one would when one meets another person for the first time. The interviewee doesn't want to jeopardize his plans of coming on board the organization, and the interviewer doesn't want the interviewee to go away having a lesser-than-stellar impression of the organization. Yet, the job interview theatric may not adequately cover the most required information to assess how well an applicant fits the advertised position. Tips on how to ask more appropriate questions were discussed.

Another popular organizational theatric that was discussed also was the idea about giving suggestions. Giving suggestions should be open and cordial, yet, it is often done theatrically in many organizations. The rational mind comes into play, preventing the giving of open and cordial suggestions. Tips on how to give suggestions within such theatrical constraints were discussed.

We also looked at diversity as an organizational theatric. Diversity is a new buzzword that organizations have embraced. Yet, organizations aren't even sure if they need such diversity, or if the diversity they bring in will meet their expectations for the future, or if this diversity will be tolerated by the other elements in the organization, such as the employees and the organizational structure. Divergence can be misconstrued for dissidence and deviance. The iron cage is for monkeys, not for divergents.

# CONCLUSION

The workplace is a war zone. Every single day, we have to face incompetent colleagues, horrible bosses and organizational theatrics. The problem with these is that they serve as a hindrance for us to realize our needs from the organization. We always have in mind a desire to maximize satisfaction and remuneration, while at the same time, minimizing effort. We do put in effort at work, yes, we do, but we are just not altruistic enough to put in unbridled effort where the returns and satisfaction may not be to our expectations. None of us wants to look for a needle in a haystack. We'd have to unbundle the hay, lay it all out, then painstakingly go through each clump of hay to look for that elusive needle that looks almost like any other strand of hay. And what do we get for that effort? One miserable needle. Made of pig iron, probably. Not worth it.

What we'd like is to put in effort commensurate with the remuneration and satisfaction we get. This is where our equation is balanced. We wouldn't mind, actually, if our equation was unbalanced on the side of our benefit. Who would complain if they got paid truckloads to have fun while not having to lift a finger? As they say about Hugh Hefner, when he finally passes away, no one will say "he's gone to a better place". The owner of the Playboy Mansion cannot possibly be better of anywhere else, can he?

Now, while most of us are going about balancing our equations, we inevitably will run into conflict with our colleagues. This is especially so because most of us are competing for the same set of resources at work. We all want tasks which give us satisfaction. We all want to be paid well. And we don't want to have to put in overwhelming amounts of effort. And when we run into conflict with each other, that's when the war starts. For

Staffers, it doesn't take a public declaration of war to run an offensive. Just look at the Gossipmongers. They use and abuse information to their own advantage. Information is used to make others look bad while they look good. That's one light offensive that colleagues often use at the workplace. Another kind of offensive that is often used a more stealthy type of offensive, used mainly by Whisperers. Whisperers, as their name suggests, gather information for and whisper information to Management. They are often given privileged status for this service done. Another stealthy type of colleague, although stealthy in a different way than the Whisperers, are the Mice. They're overly cautious, and are very afraid of offending anyone along their way. They won't openly compete with other colleagues because they are very concerned with how others see them. The Mice are quite different from the Non-Competitive Ones, though. The Non-Competitive Ones do not compete. Period. They've got all the resources they need, and so don't need to slug it out with the rest of us. Some of the Non-Competitive Ones need a different set of resources than the rest of us. They might be at the job just because they want something to do in the daytime. They're not really looking for satisfaction or remuneration in the same way the rest of us are. Other Non-Competitive Ones have their resources fed to them by their patrons. They're completely satisfied and well-remunerated, at least for the moment.

While we're all stuck in this war zone called the workplace, the Keyboard Warriors fight very differently from the rest of us. Keyboard Warriors are fearsome martial artists... behind the safety of the keyboard. They can send poison-pen emails as easily as they scratch their asses. They feel the power behind the distance bestowed upon them by the email system. I mean, they do work, these Keyboard Warriors, unlike the Captains of Incompetence. Captains of Incompetence take the cake when it comes to getting the rest of us to carry their deadweight around. Some of them just cannot perform the tasks given to them. Bless their poor souls, those Fumb Ducks. But some of them are really maintaining the effort they put in at a ridiculously low level. I'm talking about the Dazy Logs and the Actors, of course. The Dazy Logs will just not put in extra effort. The Actors will not put in effort, but will pretend that they're the busiest person on the planet.

Now, are we going to be nice to all these types of colleagues mentioned earlier? I'd be nice to a Doormat, though. Ain't nothing wrong with Doormats except that they haven't grown a spine yet. But yes, are we going to be nice to all these types of colleagues mentioned earlier? Depends on two factors. Firstly, are they in our face? Are they taking steps to make our lives difficult? Are they launching offensives our way? Have they declared war on us publicly? If so, we need to engage our opponents. But have fun at it. We can always defend ourselves by taking recourse to the legal contract that exists alongside the social contract in the workplace. We can also launch light offensives their way in a variety of ways. One thing we can do is to deny them the very resource that they need. When launching a light offensive onto a Gossipmonger, deny them of their coveted gossip, or give them misleading gossip. When dealing with Keyboard Warriors, close the distance between us and them. Approach them in person and watch their machismo fade into the background. By denying them the resources they most desire, we are doing what the behaviorists call as "negative punishment". We're denying them of stimuli which will make them less painful to deal with. Be careful of declaring war though. War is costly. War takes a toll on us, our opponents and anyone else who is involved in the war. Remember how we calculate qualitative costs? We take our salary and divide it by 365 days in a year, then divide it by 24 hours in a day. Why do I count even non-working days and non-working hours? Because we need money every single minute that we live. Every breath we take costs a pretty penny or so. We don't just spend money on food, clothing and shelter when we're at work do we? No. We have to eat, put on clothes and live under a roof even when we're not being paid.

Sometimes we need allies against another opponent in the workplace war. Always remember to make an alliance relevant to the potential ally. Don't tell them how an alliance will benefit us. That will not help our cause at all. Tell them how an alliance can benefit them instead. When they see that they're benefiting from the alliance, they're more likely to agree to an alliance.

It is not only with colleagues that we can ally. We can ally with Management as well, if it serves our purpose. But, whatever you do, do not ally with a Manager to take out another Manager. You're not going to win that battle. Management has a sense of group preservation that comes from the trust that the organization has placed in them. The organization empowers Management to represent the interests of the organization, whether it be the practices, procedures, policies or philosophy of the organization. Managers thus act like consociates with each other, and often stand in formation to defend the entire Management contingent. That is not to say that Managers do not fight against each other. They do. Even cute little hamsters fight, come on. Managers do fight against each other, but these fights occur away from the prying eyes of Staffers. Managers always maintain the Management contingent because it is their mandate to watch over Staffers and make Staffers toe the line. As such, they acknowledge that they must stand united against the Staffer hordes. Managers keep a rule between themselves regarding in-fighting. First rule of fights between fellow Managers, do not talk about fights between fellow Managers. Second rule of fights between fellow Managers, do not talk about fights between fellow Managers.

When Management stands ground against Staffers, though, they stand as being heavily weighted on defense. Managers tend to be able to defend themselves well, as well as the organization, and Staffers that seek their defense, such as Whisperers and any lousy colleague who complains about us. In fact, they tend to deploy their defenses quite readily in front of all these that they're defending. Meanwhile, they're often geared to use heavy weaponry, especially when they're mediating between contending Staffers. Management is not as limber as Staff in handling light weaponry. Staffers can do small amounts of hurt quickly, and can also use heavy weaponry to do large amounts of hurt. Remember, though, that heavy weaponry will take some amount of preparation, with costs incurred.

This is not to say that all Managers are the same though. The only similarity between Managers is that they all share the Managerial Imperative. The Managerial Imperative states that Management is most interested in maximizing productivity from and minimizing remuneration to Staffers. Quite clearly so. A Staffer who is willing to work long hours for peanuts will be appreciated by Management. A Staffer who wants to work sparingly yet demands to get paid his body weight in gold will not be appreciated by Management. Aside from this one similarity, there are many kinds of Managers. There are the Machiavellian Managers, who stand on a pedestal and piss upon us peasantry. They are the Boss, and they want us to respect their authoritahhh. Then there are the Brosses. They try to be as casual to their Staffers as possible, oftentimes treating their Staffers like their bros. They'll usually feel slighted if we don't reci-bro-cate their bromantic advances. Then there are the Simulators. Simulators manage from a distance (quite similar to Keyboard Warriors) because managing from a distance makes a lot of sense to their rational selves. They could either find solace in the distance, or they could prefer the distance because it helps them save time and effort. Among the various types of

Managers, the most confident and the most conniving has to be the Artful Dodger. Artful Dodgers are masters of being economical with the truth. They will hold back valuable information from Staffers just so that they can carry on with their own agendas. They are also able to play with semantics such that a task that no one wants to do looks like it was the most noble task on Earth. The Manager with the worst kind of luck has to be the Sandwiched Manager. He is often given the responsibility over projects but no power to make decisions or effect change. Staffers treat him like Management, yet his superior Managers treat him like a Staffer.

Now, Management represents the organization. And organizations are not always about the performance of tasks alone. Organizations are also fond of theatrics because theatrics are loud and bring organizations proud. In fact, at times, theatrics do tend to overshadow the actual real work done. Theatrics demonstrate to others the health of organizations. No point in producing good quality products if no one is going to buy them, right? Theatrics sell. With theatrics, the products and services that are produced get a nitro boost, and get noticed. In every organization, there is a work process, which sees the actual production of products and services. Yet, within this work process, theatrics exist. We see that employees neither put in their complete effort nor show their full competence in the formal work process. Employees will find shadows to hide in, lose touch with ownership of the final product and will be wary of being depended upon to continually undertake tasks, while the less competent ones sit idly by. No rational being would want to do the share of the work for someone else, while both get paid the same, right? Not unless there is satisfaction to be had, or a name to be made for oneself, you see. When it comes to these coveted tasks or projects, many rational beings will vie for a spot to contribute to it. This might look like a situation with "too many Indian chiefs", with everyone wanting to get a word in edgewise. In many organizations, however, the giving of suggestions is a privilege and not a right. Many organizations take suggestions from those of higher rank much more seriously than the suggestions given by those of lower rank. However, since asking for suggestions is a valued theatric in organizations, suggestions will still be asked for, but not quite carefully considered. The result is that the giving of suggestions will be an effort not worth undertaking.

All work and no play makes Jack stir crazy. Jack needs to stop and smell the roses once in a while too. This is where work-life balance policies come into play in organizations. Organizations are aware that employees cannot work like machines. By introducing policies that support the "life" side of an employee, organizations are hoping that productivity will increase. A rejuvenated and refreshed employee can then continue contributing to organizational productivity. Yet, how much "life" can the organization give? Organizations cannot possibly allow employees to just do whatever it is that they want to do in the name of more "life" can they? Work-life integration theatrics are a much better bet for organizations in this regard. By integrating work into life, organizations are effectively saving cost by pushing the cost of doing extra work onto the employees. Just as one would not demand to get paid for doing things that pleases one, one would not demand to get paid for every single piece of work done once work is integrated into life. Productivity goes up, cost goes down. The organization wins.

Every organization wants to sell the idea that the workplace is a family. They want every employee to believe that this idea of a family at the workplace so that they can capitalize on the emotive feelings of familial connections. Family members are not calculative with each other. Family members help each other willingly. Family members forgive each other and forget past mistakes. Family members are open with each other. Yet, the process of turning a workplace into a family is never complete. Employees do not trust each other enough to make the first move in becoming familial with each other. Employees do not trust that their fellow employees will reciprocate their trust. Any emotive friendships that occur, occur within cliques, not between every employee at the workplace.

Employees change jobs once in a while. Some, more than others. Recent findings by human resource practitioners (see articles by Cuellar in *Moneysmart* and Ho in *Channel News Asia*) suggest that staying in a job for more than 3 years at a go severely limits one's earning potential. When one changes jobs, one does so with both push and pull factors in mind. The attraction of a new job always lies in the re-balancing of one's own individual equations. One is always seeking to maximize remuneration and satisfaction while minimizing effort. Yet, at the job interview, one gives off signals that do not have any bearing on what one wants to know, which is, will this new job allow one to reduce effort while increasing remuneration and satisfaction. Similarly, the job interviewer will also be more concerned with putting the job applied for and the organization applied to in a good light, such that he is unable to discern as to whether the job applicant is able to be productive should the latter be offered the position. An applicant will be productive if he is able to competently perform tasks, and is able to fit with the organizational culture. Many organizations have downplayed the importance of their existing organizational culture as of late, in favor of attracting "diversity". Organizations seem to be keen in a workplace that has diverse thoughts, diverse skills and knowledge and diverse attitudes. As the movies *Divergent*, *Insurgent* and *Allegiant* (forthcoming) show, divergents really fit neither here nor there, because they traverse the categories that human cognition has discretely set. In fact, they might rub the organizational culture the wrong way. To celebrate diversity, organizations really need to be sure as to the sort of diverse thoughts, skills and knowledge and attitudes they really want. Organizations really need to be sure that they are attracting the correct set of divergents. Not all divergents are the same, and not all divergence points in the right direction.

We have now seen how warring the workplace can be. Alliances are made and broken. Wars are declared. Battle lines are drawn. On one side of the hill is us. We look over the hill and we see incompetent colleagues, horrible bosses and organizational theatrics. We do what we must to survive. All is fair in love and workplace war. "Yankee Rose" to you.

# ABOUT THE AUTHOR

Yasser Mattar is an organizational behaviorist based in Australia. After obtaining his Doctor of Philosophy degree from the Australian National University in 2007, he went on to provide consultation services to various individuals and organizations interested in workplace dynamics. Besides providing consultation on organizational dynamics, he has also contributed research articles to various publications, online as well as in print. His works can be found in the *Journal of International Business Studies*, *Telematics and Informatics*, and *Asia Pacific Viewpoint*, among others. He also has an alternative persona which he will leave the reader to find out more about. As he has said in this book, too much information about one's personal life can prove to be dangerous for one's professional growth. Interested readers can get in touch with him via yasser.mattar@gmail.com.

# REFERENCES

*7th Heaven.* 1996 – 2007. Spelling Television.

*Allegiant.* Forthcoming. Red Wagon Entertainment, Lionsgate and Summit Entertainment.

Arndt, Michael. 2006, 9 May. "3M's Seven Pillars of Innovation". *Bloomberg.* http://www.bloomberg.com/bw/stories/2006-05-09/3ms-seven-pillars-of-innovation

Baptiste, Ian. 2000. "Beyond Reason and Personal Integrity: Toward a Pedagogy of Coercive Restraint". *Canadian Journal for the Study of Adult Education* 14(1): 27-50.

*Braveheart.* 1995. Icon Productions, Ladd Company and BH Finance CV.

Burawoy, Michael. 1993. "Organizing Consent on the Shop Floor". In Frank Fischer and Carmen Sirianni (eds.), *Critical Studies in Organization and Bureaucracy.* Philadelphia: Temple University Press.

Burgoon, Judee K, Laura K Guerrero and Kory Floyd. 2006. *Nonverbal Communication.* Arizona: Routledge.

Burke, Lisa A., and Jessica Morris Wise. 2003. "The Effective Care, Handling and Pruning of the Office Grapevine". *Business Horizons* 46(3): 71-76.

Burns, Robert. 1785. "To a Mouse on Turning her Up in her Nest with the Plow".

Cahnman, W.J. (ed.). 1943. *Weber and Tonnies*. New Brunswick, NJ: Transaction Publishers.

Caiden, Gerald E. 1985. "Excessive Bureaucratization: The J-Curve Theory of Bureaucracy and Max Weber through the Looking Glass". *Dialogue* 7(4): 21-33.

Cathmoir, David. 1994. "Acknowledge and Use your Grapevine". *Management Decision* 32(6): 25-30.

Champoux, Joseph E. 1996. *Organizational Behavior: Integrating Individuals, Groups, and Organizations*. London: Routledge.

Cowan, Ross. 2007. *Roman Battle Tactics 109 BC – AD 313*. London: Osprey.

Cuellar, Jeff. 2014, 8 July. "Why being a "Loyal" Employee May be More Harmful than you Think". *MoneySmart*. http://blog.moneysmart.sg/career/why-being-a-loyal-employee-may-be-more-harmful-than-you-think/

Degani, Asaf and EL Wiener. 1994. "Philosophy, Policies, Procedures, and Practices: The Four "P"s of Flight Deck Operations". In N. Johnston, N. McDonald and R. Fuller (eds.), *Aviation Psychology in Practice*, pp. 44-67. Hants, England: Avebury Technical.

Dewan, Akankasha. 2015, 29 June. "Employee Engagement is no Longer HR's Top Concern". *Human Resources*. http://www.humanresourcesonline.net/employee-engagement-longer-hrs-top-concern/

Dickens, Charles. 1938. *Oliver Twist; or, The Parish Boy's Progress*. London: Bentley's Miscellany.

*Die Hard*. 1988. Twentieth Century Fox Film Corporation, Gordon Company and Silver Pictures

*Divergent*. 2014. Summit Entertainment and Red Wagon Entertainment.

Eisenbrey, Ross. 2007, 20 June. "Strong Unions, Strong Productivity". *Economic Policy Institute*. http://www.epi.org/publication/webfeatures_snapshots_20070620/

*Emirates 24/7*. 2013, 14 July. "Man divorces wife by SMS after 25 years". http://www.emirates247.com/news/region/man-divorces-wife-by-sms-after-25-years/

*Everybody Hates Chris*. 2005–2009 Chris Rock Entertainment, 3 Arts Entertainment, Paramount Network Television and CBS Paramount Network Television.

*Everybody Loves Raymond*. 1996–2005. Where's Lunch, HBO Independent Productions and Worldwide Pants.

Fletcher, Denise (ed.). 2002. *Understanding the Small Family Business*. New York: Routledge.

*Forrest Gump*. 1994. Paramount Pictures.

Fortado, Bruce. 2011. "A Field Exploration of Informal Workplace Communication". *Sociology Mind* 1(4): 212-220.

Foster, John. 2003. *Class Struggle and the Industrial Revolution: Early Industrial Capitalism in Three English Towns*. London: Routledge.

Foucault, Michel. 1995. *Discipline and Punish: The Birth of the Prison*. New York: Vintage Books.

Foucault, Michel. 2011. *The Government of Self and Others: Lectures at the College de France, 1982-1983*. Basingstoke: Palgrave Macmillan.

Freud, Sigmund. 1920. *Beyond the Pleasure Principle*. Vienna: International Psycho-Analytical Association.

*Game of Thrones*. 2011 – present. Home Box Office, Television 360, Grok! Studio, Generator Entertainment and Bighead Littlehead.

Graves, Joseph L. 2001. *The Emperor's New Clothes: Biological Theories of Race at the Millennium*. Newark, NJ: Rutgers University Press.

Guns N' Roses. 1991. "November Rain". Track off *Use your Illusion I*. Geffen Records.

Guns N' Roses. 1991. "Breakdown". Track off *Use your Illusion II*. Geffen Records.

Haden, Jeff. 2012, 20 December. "6 Reasons Why You Hire the Wrong People". *Inc.com*. http://www.inc.com/jeff-haden/6-reasons-employers-hire-the-wrong-person.html

Heath, Chip and Dan Heath. 2010. *Switch: How to Change Things when Change is Hard*. New York: Crown Business.

Herzberg, Frederick, Bernard Mausner and Barbara B. Snyderman. 1959. *The Motivation to Work*. 2nd Edition. New York: John Wiley.

*Highlander*. 1986. Thorn EMI Screen Entertainment and Highlander Productions Limited.

Hobbes, Thomas. 1651 [1886]. *Leviathan or The Matter, Forme and Power of a Common Wealth Ecclesiasticall and Civil*. London: Routledge.

*Horrible Bosses*. 2011. New Line Cinema and Rat Entertainment.

*Horrible Bosses 2*. 2014. BenderSpink, New Line Cinema and RatPac Entertainment.

*Insurgent*. 2015. Red Wagon Entertainment, Mandeville Films, NeoReel and Summit Entertainment.

Jackson, Eric. 2012, 17 August. "The 7 Reasons Why 360 Degree Feedback Programs Fail". *Forbes*. http://www.forbes.com/sites/ericjackson/2012/08/17/the-7-reasons-why-360-degree-feedback-programs-fail/

Jackson, Louise A. 2004. *The Mule Men: A History of Stock Packing in the Sierra Nevada*. Missoula, MT: Mountain Press.

James, Oliver. 2013. *Office Politics: How to Thrive in a World of Lying, Backstabbing and Dirty Tricks*. London: Vermillion.

*Japan Today*. 2015, 25 May. Working to Death in Japan: Health Warning over "No Overtime" Law. http://www.japantoday.com/category/national/view/working-to-death-in-japan-health-warning-over-no-overtime-law-2

Jo Li. 2014. "Everything Is Awesome". Track off *The Lego Movie*. Village Roadshow Pictures.

Keynes, John Maynard. 1930 [1963]. *Economic Possibilities for our Grandchildren: Essays in Persuasion*. New York: WW Thornton.

Lam, Bourree. 2015, 22 May. "New Research Suggests that Competent Employees are Assigned More Work - But they don't Always Like it". *The Atlantic*. http://www.theatlantic.com/business/archive/2015/05/being-a-go-getter-is-no-fun/393863/

Lee, Harper. 1960. *To Kill a Mockingbird*. New York: Harper Collins.

Lemert, Edwin. 1967. *Human Deviance, Social Problems and Social Control*. Englewood Cliffs, NJ: Prentice-Hall.

Levitt, Steven and Stephen J. Dubner. 2005. *Freakonomics: A Rogue Economist Explores the Hidden Side of Everything*. New York: William Morrow.

Loh, Dylan. 2015, 23 June. "Been in the Same Position for Five Years? Might be Time to Move: Experts". *Channel New Asia*. http://www.channelnewsasia.com/news/singapore/been-in-the-same-position/1933652.html

London, Jack. 1904. "The Scab". *Atlantic Monthly*.

Machiavelli, Niccolo. 1532. *The Prince*. Florence: Antonio Blado d'Asola.

*Mad Men*. 2007 – 2015. Lionsgate Television, Weiner Bros., American Movie Classics and U.R.O.K. Productions.

Mann, Charles Riborg and George Ransom Twiss. 1910. *Physics*. Chicago: Scott, Foresman and Company.

Mathis, Robert L, John H. Jackson and Sean R. Valentine. 2013. *Human Resource Management*. 14th Edition. New York: Cengage Learning.

McLuhan, Marshall. 1964. *Understanding Media: Extensions of Man*. Toronto: McGraw Hill.

Mill, John Stuart and Jeremy Bentham. 2004. *Utilitarianism and Other Essays*. Edited by Alan Ryan. London: Penguin Books.

Miner, Horace. 1956. "Body Ritual among the Nacirema". *American Anthropologist* 58: 503-507.

Nolan, Alan T. 1991. *Lee Considered: General Robert E. Lee and Civil War History*. Chapel Hill: University of North Carolina Press.

Williamson, Oliver E. 1981. "The Economics of Organization: The Transaction Cost Approach". *The American Journal of Sociology* 87(3): 548–577.

Orwell, George. 1945. *Animal Farm: A Fairy Story*. London: Secker and Warburg.

Pavlov, Ivan. 1927. *Conditioned Reflexes: An Investigation of the Physiological Activity of the Cerebral Cortex*. Translated and edited by G. V. Anrep. London: Oxford University Press.

Peirce, Charles Sanders. 1958. *Collected Papers of Charles Sanders Peirce, vols. 1–6, 1931–1935*. Edited by Charles Hartshorne and Paul Weiss. Cambridge: Massachusetts: Harvard University Press.

Powell, Gary N. 2001. "Workplace Romances between Senior-Level Executives and Lower-Level Employees: An Issue of Work Disruption and Gender". *Human Relations*, 54(11): 1519-1544.

Rance, Philip. 2004. "The Fulcum, the Late Roman and Byzantine Testudo: the Germanization of Roman Infantry Tactics?" *Greek, Roman and Byzantine Studies* 44: 265–326.

Ritzer, George (ed.). 1996. "Sociological Theory". In *Max Weber*. 4th Edition. New York: McGraw-Hill.

Robb, Peter. 1995. *The Concept of Race*. Oxford: Oxford University Press.

*Rock Star*. 2001. Warner Bros., Bel Air Entertainment, Maysville Pictures, Robert Lawrence Productions and Metal Productions Inc.

Schrodinger, Erwin. 1935. "Die Gegenwartige Situation in der Quantenmechanik (The Present Situation in Quantum Mechanics)". *Naturwissenschaften* 23(49): 807–812.

Schutz, Alfred. 1932 [1967]. *The Phenomenology of the Social World*. Translated by G.Walsh and F. Lehnert. Evanston: Northwestern University Press.

*Scrubs*. 2004. "My Common Enemy". Season 4 Episode 7. Doozer, Towers Productions, ABC Studios and Touchstone Television.

Sears, Stephen W. 1999. *Controversies & Commanders: Dispatches from the Army of the Potomac*. Boston: Houghton Mifflin Company.

*Seinfeld*. 1997. "The Serenity Now". Season 9 Episode 4. West-Shapiro and Castle Rock Entertainment.

Simon, Herbert. 1957. *Models of Man, Social and Rational: Mathematical Essays on Rational Human Behavior in a Social Setting*. New York: Wiley.

Simon, Herbert. 1976. *Administrative Behavior*. 3rd Edition. New York: The Free Press.

Simon, Herbert. 1990. "A Mechanism for Social Selection and Successful Altruism". *Science* 250(4988): 1665–1668.

Simon, Herbert. 1991. "Bounded Rationality and Organizational Learning". *Organization Science* 2(1): 125–134.

Smith, Richard. 2001. "Why are Doctors so Unhappy?: There are Probably Many Causes, Some of them Deep". *British Medical Journal* 322(7294): 1073.

Smither, James, Manuel London and Richard Reilly. 2005. "Does Performance Improve Following Multisource Feedback? A Theoretical Model, Meta-analysis and Review of Empirical Findings". *Personnel Psychology* 58: 33–66.

Snyder, Kevin C. 2013. *Empower Your Employees!: Twenty "Best Practice" Activities to Supercharge Your Staff Meetings, Employee Orientation Programs, Retreats & Staff Development Workshops!*

The Beatles. 1967. "With a Little Help from My Friends". Track off *Sgt. Pepper's Lonely Hearts Club Band*. Parlophone Records.

*The Economist*. 2009, 17 September. "Google's Corporate Culture". http://www.economist.com/node/14460051

*The Fight Club*. 1999. Fox 2000 Pictures, Regency Enterprises, Linson Films, Atman Entertainment, Knickerbocker Films and Taurus Film.

*The Hindu*. 2013, 13 October. "Millions in Modern-Day Slavery, Half in India: Survey". http://www.thehindu.com/news/international/world/millions-in-modernday-slavery-half-in-india-survey/article5243964.ece

*The Usual Suspects*. 1995. PolyGram Filmed Entertainment, Spelling Films International, Blue Parrot, Bad Hat Harry Productions and Rosco Film GmbH.

*The Wolf of Wall Street*. 2013. Paramount Pictures, Red Granite Pictures, Appian Way, Sikelia Productions and EMJAG Productions.

US Army. 1947. "Procedure for Military Executions". Manual 27-4.

Weber, Max. 1994. *Political Writings*. Edited by Peter Lassman. Cambridge: Cambridge University Press.

Yarrow, Kit. 2014. *Decoding the New Consumer Mind: How and Why We Shop and Buy*. New York: Jossey-Bass.

www.ingramcontent.com/pod-product-compliance
Lightning Source LLC
Chambersburg PA
CBHW070855180526
45168CB00005B/1834